LIFE IS AN
OBSTACLE
COURSE

LIFE IS AN OBSTACLE COURSE

*Wisdom from the book of James
on living an overcoming life*

Andrew Owen

New Wine Press

New Wine Ministries
PO Box 17
Chichester
West Sussex
United Kingdom
PO19 2AW

ISBN 978–1–905991–13–6

Typeset by CRB Associates, Reepham, Norfolk
Cover design by CCD, www.ccdgroup.co.uk
Printed in Malta

CONTENTS

CONTENTS

INTRODUCTION

You were meant to make it! It is God's intention that you reign in life.

We were called to victorious living. Paul said,

> *"For if by the one man's offence death reigned through the one,* ***much more*** *those who receive abundance of grace and of the gift of righteousness will reign in life through the One, Jesus Christ."*
> (ROMANS 5:17, emphasis added)

While history is full of people who succeeded in conquering others, they so often failed to conquer themselves. The truth is, all too often it is the ordinary, everyday things that get us down and then maybe out!

One philosopher, commenting on the improvements in our modernising world, said,

> "They are but improved means to an unimproved end."
> (Henry David Thoreau)

It really doesn't have to be this way!

One historian writing about Alexander the Great said that there came a day when he sat down with his leaders and cried! He cried because there were no more territories to take. But at the same time his body was wasting away because of sexually transmitted diseases caught through unquenchionable lust. In conquering others he couldn't conquer himself.

The book of James is such a brilliant book because it deals with the real issues of life that all of us face, day in and day out, and shows us how to exercise dominion over the many things that are pitched against us and could potentially derail us. James gives us the practical "how to's" of coming through strong so that we learn both how to conquer ourselves and at the same time become conquerors in life.

James' epistle is the earliest document of the New Testament written around AD 45. James was Jesus' half brother, born to Mary and Joseph after Jesus (along with some other kids). He was not a believer in "the Christness" of Jesus until after the resurrection, but he then went on to become a passionate, prayerful and powerful leader in the Jerusalem church.

Since it is almost certain from the clues that we get in the Gospels that Joseph died while his kids were still relatively young, Jesus, as the eldest son, would have had a hand in raising the others. James then would have seen firsthand life at its best and possibly at its worst. He may have seen Jesus deal with money problems, family business matters, health issues, relationship issues and much more. Combining these insights whilst also living through the crucifixion gives James a unique ability to teach us about life and how to live it, and about faith and how to use it. Tradition says James was called "old camel knees" due to the amount of time he spent in prayer, probably for the church he pastored and the people he cared for so much. His direct "in your face" approach leaves us with no doubt about how God sees the challenges we face and His overwhelming plan of victorious living for us in it all.

James goes through his letter dealing with one issue at a time, so let's join him now. My intention in writing this book is that you will, with me, learn how to live life as God intended and consequently not leave this world the same way you found it.

The power behind you is greater than the task ahead!

CHAPTER 1

OVERCOMING TRIALS AND TRIBULATIONS

TESTS AND TRIALS ARE A NECESSARY PART OF GROWING

"My brethren, count it all joy when you fall into various trials."
(JAMES 1:2)

Here in Glasgow, on hearing the above, you would hear said, *"Aye, right!"*

What could possibly be good, never mind celebratory, about trials? No one likes trials or tests. I mean, did you ever wake up on the morning of an exam and shout, "Yippee! Bring it on!"?

Yet we all know it is important, even necessary, to be tested. (Even Jesus was tested and, incidentally, passed with flying colours. He is the only "certified" Saviour of the world.) We are glad, for instance, whenever we visit our doctor or dentist and see that they have the all-important certificates on their surgery wall showing that they are qualified to examine us.

Or how about this:

Imagine boarding a flight for your summer holidays and, after completing the safety instructions, the stewardess says, "Ladies and gentlemen, let me introduce you to Jack, our faithful baggage handler. For more than twenty-five years Jack has done a brilliant job, but instead of getting a gold watch he really wanted a chance to fly a plane. So let's hear it for Jack today and wish him luck as he does his best!"

You would once again hear the proverbial "Aye, right!" The passengers would be fighting one another to get off that plane. No one wants to entrust their lives to a baggage handler who's never flown before. We want a thoroughly tested pilot who has passed complex exams and flown thousands of hours!

Similarly, when we are flying in turbulent skies we are glad that the aircraft we are in has been tested, passed and approved for stresses far greater than the ones we are currently encountering. It's far better for it to fail on the ground than in the air. Just like this, testing in life is necessary and we need to understand that its purpose is to make us, not break us. We are tested so that our faith will grow and we are prepared to accomplish the awesome things that God has in mind for us. Generally we are tested so that we are proven capable of handling greater respon- sibility. For some of us that may mean responsibility for others – perhaps many others – as a leader. Would you want to trust your life to an untested person? Destiny is calling us, so tests are a means to an end. They give us the strength and the tools to overcome not only today, but to handle so much more tomorrow.

I read recently about the effects that spending an extended period of time in space has on cosmonauts. The man who endured the longest stay, Russian cosmonaut Yuri Romanenko, spent a massive 326 days aboard the orbiting space station *Mir*. When he returned to earth and underwent a medical, doctors discovered that his physical frame – his skeletal structure – had begun to degrade. As a result he found doing simple things very difficult, even walking, standing, lifting objects or hugging someone.

The degradation was caused by spending too much time in a zero gravity environment. Because no pressure was being exerted on his body, his frame had begun to collapse. Dr Arkadi Ushakov of the Soviet Academy of Sciences realised that calcium loss in bones and muscle atrophy were the two main effects of prolonged weightlessness, but that they could be largely prevented by exercise.[1]

Romanenko underwent a calcium-intensive diet and a strict training regime in order to rebuild and strengthen his bones. As a result of the work they carried out on him doctors were able to introduce new ways of treating patients with bone disorders and diseases.

The analogy is easy to see and transfer to our Christian life: without some spiritual pressure and challenges we too will become weak and ineffective; our spiritual skeletons, our inner core, will end up flimsy and insubstantial. We need tests in our life to put grit into our faith. We need certain pressures because this is what keeps us strong and makes us bigger people.

Following on from James' opening statement about tests we read,

> *"knowing that the testing of your faith produces patience. But let patience have its perfect work, **that you may be perfect and complete, lacking nothing.**"*
>
> (JAMES 1:3–4, emphasis added)

That's one big goal! To be complete and having no lack. Can troubles and trials do that for you? Apparently so, if handled in the James kind of way.

DON'T GET CONFUSED ABOUT THE PURPOSE OF TESTING

Boats, planes and cars are all subjected to stress tests way beyond their normal daily operating functions. This is done to establish the margin of error, to see how things will function in an emergency situation – in the worse case scenario. But there is no point testing something to destruction so that it won't function at all. Similarly, no one is subjected to trials and tribulations continually, because that would be counterproductive and God would not allow it. But for a season God permits us to be tested because He knows it will refine and strengthen our faith and our character.

James points out that we "fall" into trials and testings and that they are for a season, but they are not the daily norm. Today, however, more than 70% of people go and seek medical help for stress-related illnesses. GPs have often pointed to work as the root cause, but very recent surveys and research show that 70% of those people who seek help (i.e. 70% of the 70%) have "life"-related stress as the root cause, not simply work-related stress. We are meant to be human beings, but we have become "human doings".

We are built with an unusual capacity to cope with so much, but pressured times are meant to be, at best, "occasional". We are a stressed-out society because we live at such a pace and we exist in the "margins" of life. I heard someone define the margin of life as "the difference between your *load* and your *limit*." We have become a margin-less society. If your load is up to your limit then you are already stressed out and it does not take a big straw to then "break the camel's back". We need some margin in our lives: space to reflect, think and get perspective.

Isaiah tells of a day when young men will fall, fail and get weary. Jesus told of a day when men's hearts would fail them through fear. This is that day. But Isaiah also told of those who "waited" on the Lord, who put time aside to spend with God, spiritual time. Our relationship with God works like a heat exchanger, an air conditioner. He takes away the heat of our living and gives us the cool air of His peace.

Many people are now in the habit of carrying two mobile phones with them or a Blackberry and have unwittingly joined the rat-race, whether they realise it or not. But as someone once said, even if you win the rat-race, you're still a rat! James here, and later in James 5, speaks to people caught up in this materialistic world. He speaks not with the soft comforting words we like to hear from our pastors, but says,

> "... *the rich man in the midst of his pursuits will fade away.*"
>
> (JAMES 1:11 NASB)

And,

> "*Come now, you rich, weep and howl for your miseries which are coming upon you.*"
>
> (JAMES 5:1 NASB)

If you are experiencing troubles and trials all the time, then you have probably taken your load to your limit and it is long past time for a revue.

It is very clear from James' teaching, however, that God's desire is for us to make it through all of our trials and troubles and come out the other side with our faith enlarged. It is never His will to see us put down or squashed by such experiences. But in case we have doubts, James follows his statement regarding the purpose of trials with this:

> *"But if any of you lacks wisdom, let him ask of God, who gives to all generously and without reproach, and it will be given to him."*
>
> (JAMES 1:5 NASB)

In other words, James says, if we are under pressure, going through a particular trial or challenge and we are not sure how to deal with it, or perhaps don't know where it is coming from, then we should just ask God for His *wisdom* on the matter. He is more than willing to give us insight into our situation and impart His thoughts to us so that we know how to handle the circumstances we find ourselves in.

James tells us that God will reward us for enduring hardship:

> *"Blessed is the man who perseveres under trial; for once he has been approved, he will receive the crown of life which the Lord has promised to those who love him."*
>
> (JAMES 1:12 NASB)

You only reward behaviour you want to encourage

The word "persevere" here does not mean that we resign ourselves to our circumstances and say, in a defeatist manner, "Well, this is my lot in life, I'll just have to suffer through it." It actually means "to reach a place spiritually where we are able to stand strong underneath the pressure and come through the trial victorious". It particularly implies coming through without lashing out at God or others, but in a manner which says "I can do this!" The reward? A crown. There are two Greek words for crown. One (*diadem*) is reserved for monarchs and the other (*stephanos*), is reserved for Olympians, i.e. the laurel given out at the games. We get the *stephanos* here, it is the hallmark of a champion of the world.

Here's an area where many people get confused. We must not think, as some mistakenly do, that the Christian life is a life exempt from trouble. Neither should we think that if we are experiencing trials then either God has abandoned us or we have sinned and made Him angry. Neither scenario is likely to be true. If we think that God punishes us by sending trials and tribulations our way then we are no better than the 40% of the population aged 25–29 years who believe in reincarnation.[2] This group of people think that anyone who is suffering now must deserve it because of the misdemeanours they committed in a previous life! No, let's not be confused. When we come into relationship with Christ we do not become immune from pressure, but He raises us up as champions through it. Remember, the power within us is greater than the challenge before us and a crown of life is promised to those who can say, "I've come though this with God's help and I have grown as a person in the process."

Many people live their lives with the thought in the back of their minds that somehow God is against them. This **may** be true! And you may need to listen to that voice and do something about it. Read the Bible carefully. While many Christians run around telling people, "Jesus loves you", they are misleading people by not giving them the full story. The truth is the Bible calls us all "children of God's wrath". Have we any idea of the effect our sin has on God, never mind each other? Logic says that if God is Holy and just, then He must have a response to sin – i.e. an angry one. You can't, at the same time, be just and holy, but then passive or indifferent to rape, murder, child abuse and genocide. God has a just reaction to such things, it is called holy anger and promises due recompense to such people. Great, we say, that's only good and proper. Let them have it! Bring it on, the sooner the better! But the picture is a little broader. We specialise in grading sin, measuring other people's actions by our intentions. But when we measure up against God's standards we *all* miss it.

Thinking lust is the same as doing it, said Jesus. God is against us all, He has to be by His very nature, but He wants to be for us! God doesn't want to wipe us out, He wants to give us life. That's the wonder of this man, Jesus. He *crosses* out our sins so that God doesn't hold them, any of them, against us any more. Once our peace is made with God, the "Emmanuel principle" kicks in: God is with us! The greatest promise God ever gave us was not even, "I'll forgive you", but "I will never leave you."

I admit, that when in the midst of a trial, it is often hard to see the wood for the trees and we can quite easily think that the reason we are in this predicament is because God is judging us. But this is generally because we still harbour the guilt and shame of sins we have previously committed, despite the fact that God has forgiven us for them. We are down on ourselves and say, "I've made so many mistakes in my life and now this is God's judgment on me..." This is never the case. God placed all of the judgment for our sin onto His Son, Jesus Christ, and if we have put our trust in Jesus and repented of our sins, then we are forgiven. We need not carry around the baggage of sins previously repented of or live any more in sin-consciousness which is so debilitating. The greater the awareness of our need, the greater the awareness of our salvation.

One of the things that the Bible teaches us is that God is totally consistent. Later in his epistle James writes that in God, *"there is no variation or shadow of turning"* (James 1:17). God is the same today as He was yesterday. He doesn't have moods and change the way He feels about us. He is not like an earthly father who might come home from work having had a good day and throw presents at his kids – but then, when he's had a bad day at work, equally might come home ranting or raving!

When trials and troubles come upon you, it isn't the judgment of God. God has laid the judgment for our sins on Christ as Isaiah 53 makes clear:

> *"Surely He has borne our griefs*
> *And carried our sorrows;*
> *Yet we esteemed Him stricken,*
> *Smitten by God, and afflicted.*
> *But He was wounded for our transgressions,*
> *He was bruised for our iniquities;*
> *The chastisement for our peace was upon Him,*
> *And by His stripes we are healed.*
> *All we like sheep have gone astray;*
> *We have turned, every one, to his own way;*
> *And the LORD has laid on Him the iniquity of us all."*
>
> (ISAIAH 53:4–6)

Do we deserve to have the judgment of God on our lives and be punished for our sin? Yes, we certainly do. But God does not give us what we deserve! Whenever we are experiencing trouble we need never listen to the voice of the enemy that reminds us of everything we've done wrong, saying, "Well, you deserve it" because God has already taken care of the things we deserve.

This is so important because if we think that God has put something in our lives on purpose, then we won't work to remove it, we'll accept it and live with it. We need to understand that at times God has simply allowed such things to be there so that we will exercise our faith and push them right out of our lives, growing spiritually in the process.

FAITH IS THE KEY

Trials and tribulations are all about growing our faith. If we are tested it is because God wants us and our faith to be stretched and enlarged. What is faith other than, at its most basic, an expression of our trust in God? Trusting in all that He has done and in all that He is. Faith is saying to God, "I trust You. I believe You. I believe You can and I believe You will."

Faith is the *one* thing that moves God. We don't get anything from God because we deserve it. He doesn't bless us because we are well connected, rich, attractive or successful. We don't get anything from God because we have kept all the commandments! And listen to this: neither do we get anything from God because we are poor, have nothing and think we deserve a break!

Faith is the only thing that moves God!

When we go through a trial, the lesson God wants us to learn is not the trial itself. The lesson to be learned is in gaining faith for the trail. It is a subtle but important difference. Misunderstand this and you will be more confused than a bunny in the headlights! Trying to work out the rhyme or reason for a trial is a fruitless exercise. The only reason for it, as James said, is to make you complete, lacking nothing. The reason is to get your faith going – and then to get that problem moving right on out of your life!

Job, who suffered a lot, had some very unhelpful friends who said to him, "You must have screwed up. God is mad at you." But he, without a Bible, a book or an MP3 download, before the cross and before Pentecost, came through with a double blessing. How? He put his trust in the goodness of God and let that goodness flow from him to his friends as he prayed for them. God does not teach us in the trial, *He teaches us in His Word and we apply it to the trial!*

> *"So then faith comes by hearing, and hearing by the word of God!"*
> (ROMANS 10:17)

So the issue is not what are we feeling, but what are we hearing?

And to be absolutely sure we get it, James warns us not to go surfing on our emotions to be tossed around like the surf of the sea, but get to the point where we are single-eyed and single-minded about who is coming through here!

James introduces himself in his own epistle as, *"James, a bondservant of God and of the Lord Jesus Christ"* (James 1:1). James was, of course, the son of Joseph and Mary and Jesus' half-brother. He became senior pastor of one of the most powerful churches in the New Testament. He could have opened his letter by saying, "I'm James, Jesus' brother." Instead he just identifies himself as a servant of God and a servant of Jesus. He knew, better than anyone, that his credentials meant nothing to God without faith.

Later James writes,

> *"Let the lowly brother glory in his exaltation, but the rich in his humiliation, because as a flower of the field he will pass away."*
> (JAMES 1:9–10)

James points out that the materially rich and materially poor are on the same level as far as God is concerned. Only their faith sets them apart from one another. Faith moves God and whether we are rich or poor, young or old, everyone of us has a measure of it to work with. James says, "Rich or poor, low or mighty, it makes no difference. It's the same ingredient that gets God moving on your behalf: your faith."

And this is what sustains us through trials and troubles.

Faith is like a muscle. When I go to the gym and pump iron, I could say to the trainer, "It's heavy, get it off me!" But he says, "You push it" and even as I push my biceps grow. Similarly, with trials and tests you have to have a contending spirit which says, "I will contend with this thing and push it right out of my life." Not only do you end up coming through, but you end up coming through stronger.

We Can Exercise Dominion Over Trials and Troubles

James insists that we should "... *count it all joy when you fall into various trials*" (James 1:2). We need to understand precisely what James means here because many people interpret this wrongly.

Some think, "Oh, that's just what Christians do, count it all joy no matter what is happening to them." In other words, they pretend to be happy when really they are miserable! This is not what James means. It is pointless to start calling bad things good and, when we are in pain, to say, "It's good, it really is!" Because that's blatantly untrue!

This kind of attitude reminds me of the little boy at Sunday School who, when his teacher asked, "What's small, grey and furry with a bushy tail?" replied, "I know the answer is supposed to be Jesus, but it sure sounds like a squirrel to me!"

Some Christians believe it's a virtue to suffer, to be in pain, to be miserable and have nothing! So rejoice, you've got some Christian virtues!

A few years back a friend of mine in his late thirties was admitted to hospital with chest pains. I went to visit him whilst the hospital were awaiting the results of tests carried out on him. He looked sick and was feeling quite low. I asked him how he was doing and at first he said, "Fine, feeling OK." But then he continued, "I'm ready if it's my time."

"What?" I said.

"Well," he continued, "I know I'm saved and I know I've got my place in Heaven. If it's my time to go, I'm ready . . . "

I was shocked! What he was saying sounded quite pious and religious, but it wasn't founded on fact or the truth according to God's Word. I said to him, "Don't you dare lie down in this thing. Get up and start fighting!" Not one of us should settle for anything less than our three score years and ten (and a whole load more besides!). I think that if my friend, at the age of thirty-eight, had given up and died the Lord would have told him when he got to Heaven, "Stand over there, your house isn't ready yet!"

In the event he made a full recovery!

The reason James says that we can count it all joy in our trials is this: God is a deliverer and God is on our side. The Bible says,

"And do not turn aside; for then you would go after empty things which cannot profit or deliver, for they are nothing. For the LORD will not forsake His people, for His great name's sake, because it has pleased the LORD to make you His people."

(1 SAMUEL 12:21–22)

Let's look at these verses in context. The nation of Israel didn't have a king because God was their King. But the people, lobbying the prophet Samuel who was God's spokesman, whinged and begged, "We want a king! We want a king like all the other nations to take us out into battle, to be our hero and champion and our deliverer!"

Samuel was upset about this because he knew it wasn't God's will. God was upset too because God takes pride in being our Deliverer. "Is the arm of the Lord shortened so that He cannot save?" God asked. Samuel advised the people that they were doing the wrong thing, but they insisted and were ultimately much worse off for it. People are powerless to deliver us, but our God is a mighty Deliverer. He takes great delight in delivering us from hopeless situations.

So when we face challenges we can call on God and rejoice because we know He is a Deliverer and He will come to our aid. God wants to step in and act on our behalf. As Psalm 60:12 puts it:

"Through God we shall do valiantly, for He it is Who shall tread down our adversaries."

(AMP)

We all face challenges where, if we exercise some strength, intellect and ability, we can overcome. But all of us face challenges that are too big for us at times and we need a deliverer. Everyone needs a Saviour to save them from their sin, because we cannot save ourselves. God takes delight in helping us when we are powerless to help ourselves. He wants us to be able to stand up and say, "God did this for me." This is the message of the Bible. We can know the Word and become experts in theology, but if we are not connected to the God of the Word our lives will be powerless.

This of course raises the huge question of suffering. Why do bad things happen to good people. Why have bad things happened to me? I could list them, lots of them. Bad things happen because we live in polluted world and it affects everything. But God is good and He is stirring up within us an Olympic champion. But doesn't the Bible promise suffering? Didn't Jesus say we would experience it? The only place I find the promise of suffering in Scripture is always in connection with persecution for my faith. That kind of suffering, said Jesus, will come my way. All other kinds of suffering are to be fought as trials to be overcome. Every sickness was challenged by Jesus. On seventeen occasions in the Gospels Jesus healed *everyone* who was present. On forty-seven occasions He healed people in ones or twos as He journeyed somewhere. There is no instance where He ever refused to heal. Prosperity is promised as a reward for following God and poverty is a curse to be avoided, plus we are encouraged to help lift others from it.

Then do we win every battle? I haven't yet, but I mean to! And even when I've lost I still win! For God is with me and comforts me and He has this knack of turning even the bad stuff into a positive contribution to my life

> *"... all things work together for good to those who love God, to those who are called according to His purpose."*
>
> (ROMANS 8:28)

CALL ON GOD AND CONNECT WITH HIM

Last, but not least, when we are caught up in trials and tribulation we must learn to always call on God. God expects this. Psalm 50:15 tells us,

> *"Call upon Me in the day of trouble;*
> *I will deliver you, and you shall glorify Me."*

What I love about God and the advice of James in this epistle is that He doesn't set out to teach us how to manage our problems. God doesn't take us into therapy and coach us how to do things differently, to understand ourselves a little better. Instead, the solution is always to know *Him* better and to know that *He* takes ownership of us and our troubles. Sometimes the most biblical prayer we can pray in any given situation is: "God, help me!" If we will call on God, without doubting, believing that He is for us, believing that He will give us wisdom without reproach, believing that He doesn't hold things against us, then He'll answer us.

Once, my wife Sue and I visited Phoenix Park in Dublin. This is a massive park consisting of hundreds of acres and the place where Pope John Paul II conducted a mass to over one million people. There is a small hill you can visit there where the Pope stood and if you climb the steps to the top there is a plaque that says, "Here Pope John Paul II conducted mass to over one million people. Be converted daily." Sue and I looked out from the top of the hill and imagined what more than a million people standing there must have looked like.

As we returned to our car we saw a dear old lady who was obviously, by the way she was dressed, devoutly religious, tracing the exact steps that John Paul took. She kept going up to the top of the hill and then came back down, up to the top, back down, up to the top, back down, praying under her breath as she was going.

What struck me about this was the fact that people who believe they need to do penance for their sins (as this lady clearly did) have not begun to understand Isaiah chapter 53. Thank God that He doesn't require us to do penance for our sins because Jesus has done it all for us – otherwise we would never be free! We don't need to do anything other than call on God and put our absolute confidence in Him.

You may protest saying, "But you don't know what I've done … " Well, He does and He still says, "Call!" "You don't know who I've hurt … who has hurt me … " It makes no difference. God still says, "Call on Me."

In 1 Peter 5:6–7 we read,

"Therefore humble yourselves under the mighty hand of God, that He may exalt you in due time, casting all your care upon Him, for He cares for you."

The key in any situation is not to be falsely humble, but simply to humble ourselves under the mighty hand of God. We have to yield to God and not yield to the circumstances, our own negative opinions or the opinions of others. If we humble ourselves before God He will raise us up.

The Bible instructs us to cast all our anxieties upon Him. How can we come through in the day of trouble and trial? By getting hold of our problem and throwing it onto the Lord. The word "casting" in this verse carries the sense of throwing a blanket over a donkey. It is the same word that is used in the Gospels to describe how a blanket was thrown over the donkey that Jesus used to ride into Jerusalem. In other words, Peter tells us, "Cast all your anxieties on Him. He's big enough to carry them."

Recently I was reminded of a story I heard when I was a child in Sunday School. An associate pastor of the church I attended, who was then in his sixties, had served as a missionary in Japan just after World War II – a time when it was very difficult to be a missionary, especially in that nation. He and his wife devoted much of their lives to building an orphanage and looking after children who had been made orphans because of the war.

He used to teach the children the Word of God and he told us that once he showed them the verse where Jesus says, "If you believe in your heart and you say with your mouth and speak to the mountain, 'Be thou removed' God will deliver you and do it for you."

A few days after he had taught them this principle, a little boy came to him and reminded him that the orphanage had been built on the backside of a hill in shade and shadow so it never got any sun. They'd been grateful to have any land and so they'd just taken what was given to them so they could build the orphanage. But the little boy came to him and said, "I would just love some sunshine through my bedroom window and I'd love some sunshine on my garden to play in. I'm going to speak to this mountain because I believe that God can remove it."

The pastor said he'd tried explaining to him that he shouldn't take the verse quite so literally, to try and work his way out of the fix that he found himself in with this little boy! But day in and day out that little boy prayed and believed. Nothing happened for about seven months until one day there was a knock on the orphanage door and standing there was an American military captain. As the pastor looked he became aware that, up the road in the distance, hundreds of troops had gathered and they had tanks and heavy earth-moving equipment. The captain was making a courtesy call to say that there was going to be a disturbance in the area for the next few months because they were building a new highway. Making the new road involved ploughing straight through the "mountain"!

Over the next four months they levelled and removed it. My old pastor said to me that he remembers the morning when the boy jumped to his feet because he was awoken by the sun penetrating through his bedroom window!

I don't know what mountain is standing and throwing a shadow over your life today, but let me assure you: our God is able and He wants to be able for you. Will you trust Him as your Deliverer?

Notes

1. Article, "The Perils of Zero Gravity", *Time Magazine*.
2. Harris poll, *Newsweek*, January 2008.

CHAPTER 2

OVERCOMING SIN
AND TEMPTATION

"Every man has his public life,
his private life and his secret life."
(Marquaz)

James has written an intensely practical book. It deals with
all kinds of issues that are relevant to everyday life. There is
no challenge in life more pervasive than that of temptation
and sin. Say what you like, man has been created a moral
being. We know what is right and what is wrong. We hate
that feeling of, "I've messed up." Yet it is a constant factor
of life. No one is immune from it. Some people get this
feeling so badly that they try to obliterate it through drink or
drugs, or, God forbid, even suicide. Others self-harm. Our

government recently reported that one in three school kids self-harm, because they feel so awful about themselves. The pain of the cut is less than the pain in their heart.

Added to this, in our "analyse that" culture, we want our problems understood more than we want them resolved. Perhaps because we resign such a mammoth issue as sin and guilt to the "unresolvable" bin. We can't figure it out so we best learn to live with it. No wonder twelve million prescriptions have been written this last year for anti-depressants in the UK alone.

But the Bible is not only timeless, it's timely. It both helps us understand and helps us resolve the problem of sin.

Here is what James has to say about it:

> *"Let no one say when he is tempted, 'I am tempted by God'; for God cannot be tempted by evil, nor does He Himself tempt anyone. But each one is tempted when he is drawn away by his own desires and enticed. Then, when desire has conceived, it gives birth to sin; and sin, when it is full-grown, brings forth death. Do not be deceived, my beloved brethren. Every good gift and every perfect gift is from above, and comes down from the Father of lights, with whom there is no variation or shadow of turning. Of His own will He brought us forth by the word of truth, that we might be a kind of first fruits of His creatures."*
>
> (JAMES 1:13–18)

TAKE A REALITY CHECK

Before we explore these verses more thoroughly and get to the heart of God's plan for beating temptation and sin, we must recognise one core truth about ourselves. It is simply this: *God is good and we are not!* No one is! We are not evolving to become a higher order of being. All the statistics point to the fact that mankind is getting worse! There are more murders, more crimes being committed, we need more police, we need to send our armed forces to more countries, we pay more insurance and we need more security measures. Every single political party campaigns on the "we will make it better" ticket because it recognises that things are not as they should be. But while our politicians may be able to change human conditions, only Jesus can change human nature.

James wants us to understand our human nature better. A correct diagnosis is essential before prescribing a cure.

Some of us feel bad about things that have been done to us, not simply the things done by us. I have, on too many occasions, sat as a pastor with people who were unable to forgive themselves for the abuse they experienced. Somehow, they concluded it was their fault. Even to these unfortunate people, James has an answer. He is giving you the explanation of where the evil came from and where the good is to come from. He is offering you, the victim, hope. Because sometimes we have to overcome both the sin done by us, and the sin done to us.

Most people realise that God is good and we are not so perfect, but those of us who have been Christians for a long while can become distant from this truth. We make much of the fact that a person is a "sinner" before he/she is saved, but have a different view of the person post-conversion.

One wrote and said this,

"Sin has a way of showing up only on the front end of salvation. Sinners are those who need to be saved, but once they are saved we rarely hear about their sin any more because, you see, they are now 'perfect' – or meant to be. Yes, it turns up in the context of all those sinners out there who desperately need Jesus. But us in here? Well, we have got saved, so do we need Him any more? It's as if we believe another standard takes over once we become Christians. Oh, the unbeliever, he receives forgiveness of sins. The believer, however, he must simply stop sinning. The blood of Jesus covered my sin when I became a Christian. But now that I'm saved, I just better straighten up and fly right. Salvation is for those who need to be saved, not those who already have been. Isn't it?"

Later the same writer says this:

"Acknowledgement of sin in our churches most often comes from those who are just being saved. We hear their stories as the equivalent of the 'before' pictures in a liposuction ad, with all that detestable flab hanging out over the edges of ill-fitting bathing suits. The assumption is that the rest of us, now we have come to Jesus, have had all the sin sucked out of our arms and buttocks and are currently enjoying our slim, trim, 'after' spiritual bodies. If sin does happen to show up later in the believer's life, it is the result of temporary backsliding and this is solved by a simple rededication of our lives to God – a sort of salvation refresher. Sin is rarely, if ever, addressed as a normal part of a believer's everyday experience."

In our reality check then we have to get past the idea that now we are saved we're not meant to face temptation, let alone succumb. It actually promotes a false sense of self-righteousness when we believe it is *only* the unsaved who are "sinners-sinning". I am convinced that many stop coming to church for this reason alone. They didn't make the grade, so they better stop meeting with those who do. Or else, they were under the illusion that they (the church) should have made the grade but didn't. Some Christians are in a worse condition than unbelievers because, not only do they still sin, but they have guilt to cope with on top! In reality maybe we should re-brand our churches as the local branch of "Christians Anonymous" and acknowledge the fact that we are all on a journey. Just as someone who is getting free from an addiction properly labels themselves a "recovering addict", so Christians should recognise they are "recovering sinners". I think Paul saw himself this way. He said,

"I discipline my body and make it my slave, so that, after I have preached to others, I myself will not be disqualified."
(1 CORINTHIANS 9:27 NASB)

Experienced addicts who have received help and have a measure of victory over their problems never refer to themselves as being "cured". They know full well that they will never be beyond the risk of succumbing again – and this knowledge plays an important part in their recovery. Sin is very much the same. We don't cease our struggle with sin when we get saved, and if we are not aware of our potential to sin then we will constantly fight a losing battle against temptation and will be forever weighed down with guilt over our failure.

Paul was unwaveringly realistic about the issue of sin in his own life. He says in 1 Timothy 1:15,

"Christ Jesus came into the world to save sinners, of whom I am chief."

When I read this scripture again recently I had to go back and re-read it. Instinctively I thought Paul must have said, "...of whom I *was* chief." But no, he describes himself as the worst of all sinners, despite the fact that he is saved and is being used mightily by God. The greatest trap of all in the Christian life is to think that God is waiting for us to become perfect before He will really love us or use us in any meaningful way. But there is nothing we can do, or not do, that will make God love us any more than He already does.

Naturally this raises the objection: "So it doesn't matter how we live then, because God will still love us?" Yes, God loves us as we are, but He loves us too much to leave us that way. His plan is to take us through a process – a process which, if we cooperate with Him, will make us increasingly like Jesus. Just realising that we have a process to go through – i.e. we're not yet the finished article and that's OK – is in itself very liberating. The Bible calls this process *sanctification*. Through sanctification God moulds and shapes us to become more and more like Him. It is a process that will continue for the rest of our lives. If we cooperate with the process then increasingly we will leave sin behind and walk closer to God. We will still have to deal with the issue of sin on a daily basis, because no matter how close to God we are, on this side of Heaven we will never be perfect – but sin will no longer control us as it once did.

CALLING SIN, "SIN"

Sadly we live in a society that is constantly trying to downgrade sin. The media always seems to be looking for ways in which to celebrate the sinful actions of others as though they were trivial "misdemeanours" or "alternative lifestyle choices", even the signs of an adventurous life. This results in numbing the collective conscience of society. Recently the Oxford University Press published a series of books on the Seven Deadly Sins. Each book, written by a different author, sets out to tackle one of the sins. *Christianity Today* magazine commenting on the books said,

> "The volumes ... channel a ... cultural tendency to metamorphose their respective sins into mere sick-nesses, and then into virtues. In Envy, for example,

[the author] Epstein diagnoses his 'sin' as just 'poor mental hygiene'. After informing us that pride is 'the fundamental sin', [author] Dyson tells us that it may well be the 'crown of the virtues' ... [author of 'Lust'] Blackburn, a University of Cambridge philosophy professor, takes a more straightforward approach in his rehabilitation of lust (not coincidentally, the fattest volume in the series). 'Lust gets a bad press,' Blackburn writes in his introduction, and he devotes the rest of the book to puffing it as 'not merely useful but essential'."

In other words, a little bit of lust does you good, gets the heart racing; a little bit of envy makes you competitive in life; a little bit of pride makes you stand up and make your mark! The world is trying to downgrade sin.

An advert that would have been confined to *Playboy* magazine in the 1950s is now a common sight in many mainstream glossy magazines. God sees things differently. Sin is sin and we need to label it as such. God wants to help us identify sin and learn to live in a place where we constantly overcome it. Sin is always negative, never positive. The Bible talks at length about it. It describes sinning as "missing the vital grade" and calls it "a power that works to pull down and destroy" and "a law that always leads to death".

For a long time I failed to see why the pages of my Old Testament were so full of blood. Blood everywhere. Sacrifices by the truck load. Blood on altars; blood on gold vessels tarnishing them for ever; blood on beautiful priestly garments stained forever. Today, we hate the sight of blood. We clean it and cover it as quickly as possible. But I realised, God used blood to tell us how abhorrent sin is to Him, the immense cost required to get rid of it, and the dire consequences of it in the human race. God hates it and so should we.

> **"He who is not angry at transgression**
> **becomes a partaker in it."**
> (C.H. Spurgeon)

GOD'S DISCLAIMER: "IT'S NOT ME!"

Look again at the words of James:

> *"Let no one say when he is tempted, 'I am tempted by God'; for God cannot be tempted by evil, nor does He Himself tempt anyone."*
>
> (JAMES 1:13)

God wants us to understand that temptation is nothing to do with Him. God does not instigate temptation since He would never want us to sin. God is good in every sense of the word – so why would He tempt anyone to sleep around or to lie? He will never do that. Notice how Jesus referred to the issue of temptation when He taught His disciples to pray: "Lead us not into temptation, but deliver us from evil." This is another way of underlining the fact that temptation is not God's idea. It is different from the trials and tribulations we spoke of in the first chapter. As far as God is concerned it is *not* part of the process of coming to maturity in Christ. God's advice is that we don't fight here, we just run, flee temptation and pray that we don't face it. The good news is that when we are being tempted, God is there with us. Hebrews 2:18 says,

> *"For since He Himself was tempted in that which He has suffered, He is able to come to the aid of those who are tempted."*
>
> (NASB)

Jesus was tempted in every way and so might we be. Jesus empathises with every kind of temptation because He has faced them Himself and so He desires to come to our aid when we are struggling.

Paul speaks in his letter to the Ephesians (2:12) of those who were *"without God in the world"*. "Hopeless" he called them. You can have God, but live as if you don't! Not only do we need God to answer prayers, or meet needs, we need Him to help us live right every moment of every day. That's why becoming a Christian is not trying to live by a new moral code, because we couldn't even if we tried. This life is beyond us! It can only be lived when we let God live His life in us and through us. I can't love my wife or my kids right unless God's love is in my heart. Never mind loving my enemies!

Not only should we call on God for help in every situation, but it will also help if we understand the biblical blueprint of temptation. God reveals this to us in James' epistle which details the process by which people are tempted and then fall into sin.

THE BLUEPRINT OF TEMPTATION

Maybe you, like me, enjoy watching the *Star Wars* movies. Remember in Episode IV when the Rebel Alliance wanted to destroy the Death Star? They needed a blueprint of this massive, planet-shaped battle station in order to see if there was any weakness in its structure they could exploit. When they finally got their hands on the blueprint – in the form of a three-dimensional hologram – they discovered that there was an inherent flaw in the design. It wasn't going to be easy, but the Alliance's war chiefs could see that if they dropped a missile into a certain portal it would blow the whole thing apart. What God has done for us in the book of James is given us the blueprint of temptation. He has shown us how to bring down this "Death Star" and blow it apart.

To use another analogy, imagine a group of biochemists who are trying to eradicate some virus or disease. They study the life cycle of the virus in order to discover what triggers it, how it develops, how it spreads and what the effects are. Similarly, God wants us to understand how temptation functions and develops into full-blown sin, so we can nip it in the bud and stop it from spreading and becoming a problem to us. The Bible is a very practical book! If you understand how temptation works you will save yourself a whole lot of heartache and start overcoming temptation and sin in your life.

James tells us that there are five steps to the temptation process:

1. Desire
2. Doubt
3. Deception
4. Disobedience
5. Death

"But each one is tempted when he is carried away and enticed by his own lust. Then when lust has conceived, it gives birth to sin; and when sin is accomplished, it brings forth death."
(JAMES 1:14–15 NASB)

Sin begins with a desire. When you allow that desire to become strong in your heart, you begin doubting what God has said about the situation you are in. After that you begin to fall into deception and actually believe you are going to derive some benefit from your intended actions. Once you believe that your "needs" will be met then you inevitably act upon your belief and end up being disobedient towards God. The Bible says that habitual disobedience to Him results in death – spiritual death if not literal, physical death. Sin always has a consequence. Wherever sin occurs, something dies. It could be a relationship, a job, a reputation, or an opportunity – but something always dies, and the process begins with desire.

It was like this way back in the beginning. The devil came along to tempt Eve. He showed her some fruit that she knew was forbidden and she desired it – she just had to have it. She doubted what God had said when the devil asked her, "Did God really say . . . ?" and he deceived her by lying, saying: "You'll be just like Him." Eve disobeyed and she died spiritually from that moment. The process that leads to sin is as old as the earth itself! The devil is still following the same handbook of "How to lead someone into temptation" today. His method has not changed. The first step is always to arouse an ungodly desire for something that God has forbidden because He knows it is not good for us.

Doubt is the next step in the process. Having had our desire stirred we look for a way to get that desire fulfilled, even if we know it's inherently wrong. We do this by questioning what God has said and compromising our conscience. We make excuses like: "It's not *really* a sin . . ." or "I'm still not as bad as so and so . . ." Or we may find "positive" excuses for doing what we want to do. For instance, if we want to indulge ourselves in some way we'll tell ourselves, "Well, God wants me blessed, doesn't He?" The truth is God does want you blessed, but He does not want you blessed more than He wants you to be responsible. God wants you to be fulfilled in your relationships, for instance, but not at the expense of infidelity to your husband/wife. You can see how doubting God's truth because of a desire quickly leads to the next step in the process: deception.

The ultimate deception is when we tell ourselves, "If I have that/do that then it will make me happy . . . more complete … a better person … fulfilled … etc. So many Christians fall into this trap. We tell ourselves, and actually believe that, if we have/do "x" we will be fulfilled and satisfied. The truth is, only God can truly satisfy all our needs. We must focus on Him as the source of our fulfilment. Once we fall into deception this quickly leads to disobedience. Once we are literally convinced that a particular course of action will meet our needs then we will pursue it.

This is all part of the blueprint of sin and the key element in it all is desire. This is why single people should be careful not to arouse sexual passion in their life. Sex is great, inside marriage, but when you are single you can't fulfil that desire without disobeying God, so the best thing to do with your desire is to keep a lid on it. Don't look at the wrong stuff or read the wrong stuff that will awaken and stimulate that desire. Don't misuse your imagination. If you can get a handle on something at the desire stage, seldom will it become a problem for you later.

WHAT CAN I DO?

So what are some practical steps we can take to deal with temptation and begin to eradicate sin in our lives? There are four important principles that will help us:

1. Be aware that everyone is tempted and no one is immune

In our earlier reality check we noted the fact that we are bound to sin from time to time simply because "God is good and we are not". I'm not suggesting that we should spend all our time focusing on our potential for sinning, but we do need to be constantly aware of our vulnerability and take steps to protect ourselves.

I remember complaining to the Lord a little while back. My complaint went like this: Lord, it's not fair that you hold me responsible for what Adam did. If he hadn't eaten off that tree, we'd all be OK! How come I'm responsible for what he did?" It was one of those moments when the Holy Spirit spoke straight into my heart and His reply was this: "Son, every person still has a 'tree in their garden' and every person has something in which they are weak." What is your tree?

Those words impacted me deeply and then I understood: each of us is different and each of us is equally prone towards sin in our own way. The fruit of the tree in the Garden of Eden was not as important as the fact was that it was "forbidden". Each of us has "forbidden fruit" that is a problem for us. I may be able to manage my diet easily without thinking about it, but maybe that's a problem for you? Maybe you can keep your cool under any circumstance, but maybe I have a problem with my temper? Maybe you are brilliant at budgeting your finances and have it all accounted for down to the last penny, so you can't understand people who spend recklessly? The fact is, each of us has a "tree". We know full well we shouldn't go near it, but often we do. We need to live with an awareness of the dangers of sin and stay away from the "tree".

2. Know the patterns

The second principle we can learn to help safeguard ourselves from temptation and sin is to recognise the patterns that lead us into sinful behaviour. The enemy knows what things can trigger sin in your life because he has taken a good look and examined your weaknesses. The enemy knows your vulnerable points and would love to exploit them if he can. Therefore it is critical that you understand the pattern temptation takes in your life and counter any ungodly desires before they progress further. Simply not putting yourself into any situation that will cause these desires to arise is a great defence. Ask yourself, "What circumstances make me vulnerable? Am I making any bad choices that are setting me up to fail?"

Imagine this scenario: you stay up late when the rest of your family has gone to bed. You have worked so hard all day and it's your time to chill and relax. You deserve it! You have all the Sky movies and other channels to yourself and you begin to channel hop. Immediately you are vulnerable. You catch a glimpse of something inappropriate on a particular channel, it catches your attention and begins to draw you in. Instead of skipping to something more suitable to watch or, better still, turning the TV off and going to bed, you find yourself continuing to watch and you've been snared. Very, very soon, watching is not enough.

What about this scenario: you go on holiday and leave your Bible at home and so you miss having any kind of time alone with God. Before you know it you are thinking things and doing things that you wouldn't do if you were keeping close to God. Maybe you begin to think, "No one from the church will see me, so I can do what I like!" Maybe you think you can knock the booze back, hit on the women/men, repent on the plane trip home and then be in church on Sunday as normal!

How about this scenario: you work late in the office on your own. You want to be diligent in your work and hope to get a promotion – at least that's what you keep telling yourself. The problem is, the girl who works in your office (who you quite like the look of), also works late and it gives you an excuse to spend more time around her. You begin to chat and sympathise with one another over all the hours you both put it. Before you know it, one of you has suggested a quick drink after work and one thing leads to another.

Only you can say where your vulnerabilities lie, so you need to talk openly to God about them and ask for His help. Every sin has a pattern and people are fairly predictable when it comes down to it. Stand back and look honestly at yourself, recognise the pattern sin takes in your life and make some right choices to avoid walking those paths. Breaking the habit patterns that lead to sin will help you to conquer the sins themselves. Sin can often be overcome by a change of lifestyle – by establishing a new pattern.

3. Be aware of where you focus your thoughts and avoid fixations

The battle for sin is won or lost in the mind. If you continually say to yourself, "I will not eat chocolate today . . . I will not eat chocolate today . . ." what are you focusing on? Chocolate! So what does that make you want more than anything else? If you use this approach to try to avoid something, you will end up fixated by the very thing you want to avoid. Maybe you grew up with parents who were dysfunctional in some way and you have constantly told yourself, "I will not turn out like my mother!" Then guess who you find yourself becoming like? Your mother. Why? Because your focus is in entirely the wrong place and you have developed a fixation on the *negative* instead of reinforcing alternative, positive behaviour patterns that will help you to be different.

Formula One racing drivers are taught to drive at very high speeds by focusing precisely on where they want to go. Everything else is kept in their peripheral vision because, as one driver said, "If you look at it, you'll hit it." It's the same with sin and temptation. Don't make the sin you want to avoid your main focus, focus on God instead. The devil likes to try and get us into a debate with him about sin and when we do, we always end up sinning. Don't have a debate about sin. Let me give you this advice: if the devil calls you wanting a chat, hang up!

Hebrews 12:1–2 affirms where our focus should be:

"Therefore we also, since we are surrounded by so great a cloud of witnesses, let us lay aside every weight, and the sin which so easily

ensnares us, and let us run with endurance the race that is set
before us looking unto Jesus, the author and finisher of our
faith . . . "

Our focus needs to be always on Jesus. Every time your
heart is focused on a particular desire that it shouldn't be –
snap out of it and focus on God.

4. Shut doors

In the Old Testament Job has a technique for countering a
particular temptation and sin. In Job 31:1 he says, *"I have*
made a covenant with my eyes; why then should I look upon a young
woman?". Job had resolved to "shut the door" on temptation
before it became a problem for him. If you are a man, how
about making a covenant with *your* eyes? We all know that
there is a difference between looking and *looking,* don't we?
The moment you become aware that you are looking at
someone inappropriately, you need to look away. It is
shutting the door on temptation. Whatever your particular
weakness is, resolve to shut the door on it.

5. Be accountable

Adam was there for Eve. He should have said, "Hang on, this
is wrong." Unfortunately he chose to sink with her, and the
rest, as they say, is history. Everything God made in Genesis
He declared to be good, except man being alone. You can't
make it on your own. If you are stuck on an issue, find a good
mate, someone who knows how to be discreet, a person who
has made it in the area that you want to come through on and
open up. Make yourself accountable to them.

WHERE IS GOD WHEN I'M BEING TEMPTED?

It isn't pleasant to be tempted and often the struggle with
temptation can leave us feeling tainted, but we must

remember that temptation is not sin. God is right there with you whenever you are tempted and He can work things out for you if you call on His help.

Paul wrote, *"all things work together for good to those who love God, to those who are called according to His purpose."* Some of us have rewritten that text in our minds so that it reads: "God will always make a happy end out of every situation." That's not what the Bible says. Neither does the Bible say, "God will work all things together for good, just the way you want them." But God will works things together for our "good". Though being tempted is tough and unpleasant, God is able to bring something positive and wholesome out of the experience. God's plan is to use every circumstance to make us more like Jesus – and temptation is no different.

A silversmith was once asked, "How do you purify silver?" He replied, "I heat it, heat it again and then heat it some more. The more I turn up the temperature the more the impurities come to the surface, and then I can skim them off." He was then asked, "How do you know when the process is finished?" He replied, "I know the silver is completely pure when I can see my face in it." Even the stuff which goes on in our lives which doesn't seem good, God can use to make us like Him. The more like Him we become, the more we are able to reflect His image to others. This is the whole point of our life's journey: to become more like Christ.

Is God there when we are being tempted? Yes, He is, because the Bible tells us He provides us a way of escape whenever we are tempted. 1 Corinthians 10:12–13 says,

"Therefore let him who thinks he stands take heed lest he fall. No temptation has overtaken you except such as is common to man; but God is faithful, who will not allow you to be tempted beyond what you are able, but with the temptation will also make the way of escape, that you may be able to bear it."

The Bible promises there is always an escape route from sin, so we must always look for it! Joseph, when Potiphar's wife tried to seduce him, took the emergency exit and ran. Sometimes the bravest thing you can do when tempted is simply to run. God wants us to get ourselves away from temptation as fast as we can. Temptation is always thought of as the opportunity to do wrong, but have you ever thought of it as the opportunity to do right? When you are being tempted to do something wrong, ask yourself, "What is the opposite 'right' thing to do here?" and then do it!

Bad habits are difficult to stop. But good habits are easier to build. Build a pattern of behaviour for twenty-one days and you will have a new habit. Maybe make it a habit of getting to bed early, rather than stopping up watching late night TV. You will get up earlier, feel better and change your whole lifestyle.

> Sow a thought reap a word
> Sow a word reap an action
> Sow an act reap a habit
> Sow a habit reap a character
> Sow a character reap a destiny

So that's where it came from!

Earlier we spoke about overcoming both sins we commit and sins committed against us. James makes it clear. He answers the question we have all been asking: "If there is a God, why is there all this evil in the world?"

Well, he told us straight. It is our own evil desires being unleashed. All good things come down from God. Evil comes up from hell through the corrupt conduit of the human heart. The heart needs saving and then offering back to God as a conduit for life from a different source.

"Therefore I urge you, brethren, by the mercies of God, to present your bodies as a living and holy sacrifice, acceptable to God, which is your spiritual service of worship."

(ROMANS 12:1 NASB)

Your success in overcoming sin is only as effective as and in direct proportion to your life given in pursuit of a good cause. Stopping never works, starting does!

As we realise that all evil comes from fallen and corrupt hearts, we must respond appropriately to evil we feel and experience.

Firstly never, ever blame God. It didn't come from Him! James has told us that. Blame Him and you will cut off the very place you will find the most help.

Secondly, don't blame yourself. James said, *"He* [God] *brought us forth by the word of truth"* (James 1:18). God wanted you here. Even before the world began you were a divine design in the mind of God. Don't live in the shadowy world of regrets and if only's.

Thirdly, know the true power of forgiveness – to forgive yourself and others.

So many think that when they become Christians they get a nice white suite called "righteousness" and they run around telling every one about it. But in no time at all they have got it dirty. They try to keep it clean, but the white at best becomes grey; confidence in prayer wanes; faith is just a thought, an idea, but no longer a way of life.

However, this illustration is flawed because God does not give us a white suit, He *is* our white suit! One of the names by which God is identified in the Old Testament is *Jehovah Tsidkenu* which means "The Lord my righteousness". Every time God sees you he is *not* sin aware, for everything you have asked Him to forgive He remembers to forget! Some find this very hard to grasp or even accept, but God really does not see your sin. He can and only does relate to you through the perfect person of Jesus. All that He is you have now become!

Don't forget to forgive either. For others like you need, and will always need, help.

> **"He who cannot forgive others**
> **breaks the bridge over which**
> **he himself must pass."**
>
> (George Herbert)

CHAPTER 3

OVERCOMING
DECEPTION

"The trouble with me
is that I am in tune with Chaos."
(Anon)

The dictionary defines *deception* as "a trick or illusion, misleading information, or a false impression given either by a statement, appearance or influence".

Some years back I bought a car which had an on-board computer, which was novel in those days. One Sunday morning I set off very early for a speaking engagement. It was a cold and frosty day and the chilly air soon woke me up from my sleepiness. As I entered the motorway some fifteen minutes later I checked the computer for the outside temperature. It read 5° Centigrade. "Funny," I thought, "must have warmed up very quickly."

I thought no more of it until at 70mph my car spun helplessly out of control, hit the central barrier and turned over on its side, continuing to slide for another quarter of a mile down the motorway. Although my car was in a very sorry state, fortunately I was okay. Sliding on the ice as I pulled myself out of the wreck I was soon made aware that it was in fact 4° Centigrade. When the garage later looked at my car they informed that the computer had been wrongly calibrated. It's starting point was wrong and so the information it gave me was wrong. I had taken the information as truth and responded accordingly. In short, I was deceived!

James writes,

> *"So then, my beloved brethren, let every man be swift to hear, slow to speak, slow to wrath; for the wrath of man does not produce the righteousness of God. Therefore lay aside all filthiness and overflow of wickedness, and receive with meekness the implanted word, which is able to save your souls. But be doers of the word, and not hearers only, deceiving yourselves. For if anyone is a hearer of the word and not a doer, he is like a man observing his natural face in a mirror; for he observes himself, goes away, and immediately forgets what kind of man he was. But he who looks into the perfect law of liberty and continues in it, and is not a forgetful hearer but a doer of the work, this one will be blessed in what he does. If anyone among you thinks he is religious, and does not bridle his tongue but deceives his own heart, this one's religion is useless. Pure and undefiled religion before God and the Father is this: to visit orphans and widows in their trouble, and to keep oneself unspotted from the world."*
>
> (JAMES 1:19–27)

The Bible has a great deal to say about deception and about things that appear to be something which they are not.

Riches, it says, are deceptive, so we mustn't set our heart on them. They promise satisfaction but leave us empty. Sin is the ultimate impostor: it entices us to participate in its activities, offering pleasure and promising a great deal that it cannot deliver. The Bible also warns us that we can be self-deceived and to add to the challenge we are told that there are evil spirits at work which it calls "seducing spirits", always enticing and misinforming us in their untiring attempt to lead us up the garden path.

What we think about a particular issue is extremely important. Think about this: how do you control the direction of a ship? By using its rudder, of course. How do you control the direction of a space rocket? By booster rockets I am told. Fire them in one direction and you go in the other. How would you control the direction of a horse? By the bit in its mouth and the bridle on its head. So, how do you control the direction of a human being? The direction a person takes in life is determined by their thoughts, which in turn form their beliefs and convictions. Scripture confirms this for we read,

"For as he thinks in his heart, so is he."

(PROVERBS 23:7)

It is vitally important, therefore, that the beliefs we base our lives on are true and in line with the Word of God, and that they are constantly checked and monitored. Not some but *all* of our actions are based on our beliefs. Beliefs motivate actions.

Note also the verse does not say, *"what* a man thinks", but *"as* a man thinks". Contrary to the counsel of some life coaches, positive thoughts are not enough. It's not *what* we think but *how* we think that counts. You can get pumped up in a church meeting and walk out of the door feeling good. But if you return to the pattern of, "it applies to him, but not me" your feelings of wellbeing will be short-lived. Others' lives are motivated by thought patterns such as, "it's just not fair" or "I was never wanted, never needed" or even simply "I can't..." The truth is, if you continually tell yourself, "I can't" then you never will. You were designed to walk in agreement with your thoughts. Truly,

---

"The thought is ancestor to the deed."
"Men don't rule the world – thoughts do!"
(Disraeli)

Back in the late 1950s psychologists coined the term "cognitive dissonance" – cognitive meaning "concerning our thought processes" and dissonance meaning a "lack of consistency or compatibility". Cognitive dissonance describes the uncomfortable feeling a person has when they act in a way they know is in conflict with their beliefs. In other words, if you attempt to do something but believe the opposite you will not succeed. This explains a lot. Faith operates in this way. When we become fully convinced of a truth it will be realised in our life. Billy Graham said that success came in his ministry when there was no longer a gap between what he thought in his head and spoke with his mouth. At that point everything took off.

But before we move on, consider this:

The most common title given to Jesus was "teacher", yet He never had one pupil, only disciples. What's the difference? A pupil thinks he has learned something when he can repeat it, but a disciple knows he has learned something when he can do it, and thinks the pupil is deceived if he only believes it. It's not about *information*, but about *formation*. Going on that basis, we could say half the church is deceived, for it already knows considerably more than it is living!

The word that we translate "deceived", a word James uses on two occasions in these few verses, means to "misreckon" or "miscalculate" and so be deluded. In other words, it describes a scenario in which we base our judgments on false information and as a result make miscalculations that have a detrimental effect on the course of our lives.

Recently I read about the concerns some UK aviation experts have about long-haul flights entering Britain. Aviation fuel is so expensive that many airlines ration fuel, giving their planes just enough fuel to make it to their destination. Experts feared that, in peak periods when numerous planes are wanting to land, these planes would not have enough fuel to circle the airport for the required time until they are given a landing slot. The implication was that an aircraft might come crashing down over the city of London as it ran out of fuel if there was even the slightest miscalculation in planning. Miscalculations can have catastrophic consequences.

The dictionary also defines *deception* as "an impostor" – i.e. something (or someone) pretending to be something that it is not.

Many years ago, my grandfather spent much of his working life trying to carve out a living for himself, his wife and their twelve children on a mountainous area of Wales. These mountains were bleak in winter and the soil very thin. My grandmother was a passionate Christian and it was largely through her that I and others in our family found Jesus. Although my grandfather didn't always appreciate her evangelical zeal, he nevertheless had strong principles, and each of his sons ended up learning a useful trade, which was a big deal seventy years ago.

But there came a moment when they could no longer continue to live and work on these mountains and so they prepared to move into a little cottage down in the village. In the process of moving they unearthed a terrible truth.

When they took on the smallholding many years before, there apparently turned up a man who said, "I'm the landlord, I own this land and this is how much you're going to have to pay in rent to work this ground." In those days in Wales most business transactions took place on the basis of a handshake and your word was your bond. There was no documentation and hardly anyone knew a lawyer, let alone had access to one. So every January this guy turned up to collect the annual rent, rent for the house and additional rent for the land. Sometimes giving gifts out to the kids, all smiles.

Many years passed by and on the day they moved from there my grandfather discovered that the man to whom he had been paying rent for these many years never actually owned the land, just the cottage. It wasn't his land, it was in fact owned by no one, it was common land, but it was too late by then to do anything about it. They had been deceived by this impostor who had been taken at face value. They believed his tale and so paid their dues. I don't know how much they paid out, but any amount was too much.

In a similar way, many of us live our lives paying dues to others when we don't need to. Deception does that. It is a tyrant and a thief, not just stealing our peace and possessions, but life itself as we try to live it.

Some are paying dues to the devil. He's got them trapped in fears or phobias, constantly anxious and emotionally bound up and they are living life under the misapprehension that this is as good as life gets, just accepting it.

Others are paying religious dues, living life like the old school report, "must try harder, can do better!"

How about this? A "pastor" moved into a local city a few years ago to pioneer a church. Like other ministers he had been marrying people on a regular basis for three of four years, when it was discovered that he was not licensed to do so. The terrible consequence of this deception was that the people he had "married" were not married at all. The people affected by this, especially those who were Christians, naturally were devastated to find out.

Sometimes we can be deceived by mad ideas or strange doctrines. In the middle ages the clergy were often guilty of selling "indulgences" – religious knick knacks, novelties or certificates – saying that each indulgence would buy a few days less in purgatory for you or your family. Some TV evangelists are more or less doing the same thing today. I heard one guy say a few months ago, "Sow into this ministry and you will get your partner for life." And people did! No wonder God inspired a prophet to say, "My people perish through lack of knowledge." Not only do these people bring the Gospel into disrepute, but they tie people up in false promises and pretences. Every time I've heard Dr Billy Graham interviewed he often says, "The Bible says ... " Good advice.

MANY TYPES OF DECEPTION

Relationships and material possessions

We can be deceived in all kinds of ways. One type of deception is thinking that happiness can be found by gaining something or someone. People tell themselves, "If I could just get that job ... that car ... that pay rise ... that breakthrough ... then I'd be happy." The truth is, even if all those things happened for us we still wouldn't achieve lasting happiness. Once the chase was over and we had acquired what we wanted, then we would begin to look for the next thing. Happiness is not what happens to you but what happens *in* you!

Being single is not a disease and marriage is not the cure. If two empty people come to a marriage they are not going to make a full marriage. If we live under the illusion that those things will bring us complete happiness, we are going to be disappointed. We were only ever meant to find true happiness in one place – our relationship with God! That's how we were made, and that's why we were made.

> *"You shall love the LORD your God with all your heart, with all your soul, with all your strength, and with all your mind, and your neighbour as yourself."*
>
> (LUKE 10:27)

Prophetic words

Some believers are deceived because they spend their lives chasing after prophetic words which they hope will give their lives direction. Instead of connecting with God they are looking to others to speak into their lives. Now, I believe in prophecy. It is a gift of the Holy Spirit and the Bible tells us not to despise prophetic utterances. I am also grateful for many prophetic words I've received over the years that have confirmed the word of God to me. But I have rarely found direction for my life from a prophetic word. I have never decided to start a church or left a church, or appointed leaders, or taken a major course of action because of a prophecy. Prophecy is given for some very important things – but if you're looking to it for major direction then you need to be very, very careful.

1 Corinthians 14:3 tells us exactly what prophecy is given for:

- Edification
- Exhortation
- Comfort

Many live in disappointment because prophecy they received in good faith has not come to pass, most likely because it did not originate with God in the first place. The apostle Paul taught that every prophecy, regardless of who brings it, needs to be weighed. If anyone gives you a "word from the Lord" you must check it out properly. Prophecy is for edification, exhortation and encouragement, not usually direction. It gives us hope as we pursue what God has set before us, but we don't build our lives on it. If your life is revolving around a particular prophecy you've been given, then you are already in danger. Every word must be weighed otherwise we can be deceived.

Direction best comes when the "5 C's" line up in our lives:

- Conviction from the Holy Spirit
- Confirmation from the Word of God
- Counsel of godly people
- Consolation of the peace of God in it
- Causeway or a door to walk through

Money

We can also be deceived by money. I'm not talking here about those who are intent on making a pile of it thinking it will make them happy. I am speaking of Christian ministries that become focused on money and lose sight of their original ministry goals. Over the last few months I have seen several programmes on Christian television that said something like this: "I want to tell you that God's hand is on this ministry. If you give into this ministry there is an anointing here for you to have a double-fold measure in return ... there is an anointing on this ministry for you to have hundredfold increase..." etc.

Whoever says that is already going much further than God's Word and our spiritual alarm bells should be ringing. Some will protest, "Doesn't the Bible promise a thirtyfold, sixtyfold and even hundredfold increase? Didn't Jesus talk about that?" Yes He did, but the first rule of Bible interpretation is this: always put the text in its context or you'll have a pretext. If you take the text out of "context" you're left with a "con". When Jesus talked about thirtyfold, sixtyfold and hundredfold increases He was talking about proclaiming the Gospel. The increase referred to seeing people saved, a harvest of souls – that was the context. Although He talked about managing finances a lot in His ministry, in this instance Jesus was not talking about money. The Bible teaches us regarding tithes and offerings and about providing for those who are poor or vulnerable, but nowhere does it promise portions and increases and this kind of thing. This kind of teaching is deceptive, promising us something that goes beyond God's plan. God does promise increase on giving, He said He would pour out more than we can contain, and that is a lot!

We were not called to failure, but we were not called to success either, we were called to significance. There is a subtle difference. Chasing success materially or otherwise isn't where it's at. But when we want to truly make a difference, success isn't far away. It is safe to say that God is good. It is safe to say you will never out-give Him. It is safe to say sowing works. But it is also safe to say we are changed into champions not by the removing of our brains but by the renewing of our minds (Romans 12:2)!

Maturity

We can be deceived about our understanding of the process by which we come to a place of maturity in Christ. Every believer wants to be mature and established in their faith, but how that process occurs is very important. It matters how we deal with issues in our lives and how we cope with things when they go wrong. We have a habit of getting wrapped up and wallowing in our problems, dealing with them very badly. Often we suffer from victim-itis, but God wants to help us get to a different place.

As a kid, my life was a mess, totally and utterly screwed up. All kinds of stuff happened to me that God had to help me through. Sometimes today I smile when I counsel people and they say to me, "You won't understand what I'm going through . . . " Most of the things I hear about I have already experienced first-hand.

I came to know Jesus in my teenage years and when I met Him I was angry. I wanted to kill some people because I was hurt and confused. I managed to hide most of this under an uncommunicative personality, leaving people thinking I was quiet or thoughtful. The truth was, I was afraid that if I began speaking about how I saw things, I wouldn't be able to control my anger. But as I began to walk with God He had such simple ways of dealing with issues. I'd begin to complain about what had happened in the past and how I was the way I was because of what had happened to me, but the Lord would guide me to a place in Scripture that would say, "Forgetting the things that lie behind, I press forward to that which lies ahead."

I realised early on that God's way of dealing with issues is not the same as a psychiatrist's or psychologist's way of dealing with issues. These people are concerned with reviewing and minutely examining every detail of the past to find causes and effects. No doubt some people have been helped by this, but the Gospel has much more power to transform a person's life!

I would say to God, "These people did this to me!" and He would say, "Forgive them." I would protest, "Well, that's OK, Lord, two little words, but it's easier said than done! You don't know what they did!" "You don't know what they did to Me," God would reply, " . . . to My Son. Forgive them." And in one action it was possible to release twenty years' worth of baggage: "I forgive them, Lord . . . "

At other times I came to the Lord and said, "You don't know what I've done!" and He said to me, "If you confess your sin, I'm faithful and just and I'll forgive you. I'll cleanse you. It's done."

The further I went with God the more I realised that life with Him is really simple, it's not complex. We try to make our relationship with Him so complicated, but when it comes to growing in maturity in Christ, if we listen to what He says we can walk into the life that He has already prepared for us. The truth is, most people want their problems understood more than they want them resolved. They want people to acknowledge their pain more than they want an answer. In short, they are happier to live in deception, accepting a pale imitation of the Christian life, than they are to embrace the truth.

Doubts concerning salvation

Other Christians live with their lives clouded by a constant doubt concerning their salvation It is very common for Christians to question their salvation and ask themselves, "How do I know that I'm definitely saved?" or "Can I lose my salvation?"

I have on several occasions prayed with believers who think they have committed what the Bible calls the "unforgivable sin". Jesus defined this as "blaspheming against the Holy Spirit". And it is true to say that Jesus Himself said there is no forgiveness for this. But what is it? In my mind I am absolutely convinced that if you still have breath in your body, you have as yet not done this. To blaspheme the Holy Spirit is to decry His work, and His work is to tell you that you are a sinner and that you need a Saviour, and there is only one certified Saviour of the world – Jesus Christ. Reject Him and you will face eternity lost, without hope, and you will then have committed the unforgivable sin and will have stepped into eternity lost forever.

One indication that we are saved is that when we sin we can no longer get away with it, because the Holy Spirit convinces us of a better way, to reach for the high life instead of settling for the low life. If you continue to sin and have no conscience about it then you might be right to question your salvation. J.I. Packer once said that the only proof of past conversion is present convertedness.

The fact that God takes the trouble to discipline us is another indication that we belong to Him. Deuteronomy 8:5 tells us,

> *"Know then in your heart that as a man disciplines his son, so the LORD your God disciplines you."*
>
> (DEUTERONOMY 8:5 NIV)

This is confirmed in Hebrews 12 where we read,

> *"And you have forgotten the exhortation which speaks to you as to sons:*
>
> *My son, do not despise the chastening of the LORD,*
> *Nor be discouraged when you are rebuked by Him;*
> *For whom the LORD loves He chastens,*
> *And scourges every son whom He receives.'*
>
> *If you endure chastening, God deals with you as with sons; for what son is there whom a father does not chasten? But if you are without chastening, of which all have become partakers, then you are illegitimate and not sons. Furthermore, we have had human fathers who corrected us, and we paid them respect. Shall we not much more readily be in subjection to the Father of spirits and live?"*
>
> (HEBREWS 12:5–9)

God is a perfect Father and if we sin persistently He may well take us in hand and discipline us. Sinners sin and they have fun while they're doing it! You can look at their lives and see them having a whale of a time – they couldn't care less. But the moment a person comes to Jesus and is born again, sin troubles them. It's not that they no longer sin, because we are all prone to it, but when we do sin, it bothers us. If we persist in our sin or in our foolishness then God might have to discipline us because He loves us and truly wants the best for us, believing in us that we will come to our fullest potential because we're part of His family now.

But even in this deception looms large. We get confused between God's discipline and terrible circumstances, thinking that one is the outworking of the other. I think it a terrible teaching when some believe that God will chastise with sicknesses, accidents or diseases. The constant comparison in the Bible is that of fathers and sons. I have five sons and love each of them. I would never dream of inflicting such terrible things on my kids, so how much less would God? But I am often teaching, encouraging, correcting and training my sons. It's important to rightly divide the word of truth.

That God follows us, rather than us following Him

Another common deception in the Christian life is that once we are saved it is God's job to follow us rather than us following Him. It sounds crazy, but this is how a lot of people live. They walk along pleasing themselves. If, as a result, they end up struggling or unhappy they call on God, saying, "Come on, Lord, help me out!" It's like saying let's rub the lamp and Genie Jesus will appear. People behave like God is a maid, following them around with a dustpan and brush to scoop up the trails of destruction they leave behind them! Instead we have to learn to follow God and to walk in obedience to His Holy Spirit who guides and leads us.

I think this happens because people harbour the illusion that somebody somewhere owes them something. But in reality, if Jesus never did another thing for us, we should be eternally grateful for what He's done already. We follow Him because He is the way, the truth and the life. He will never lead us into error or deception. God is not deluding us when He tells us that He is the God who heals us. He is not deluding us when He tells us that He forgives our sins. He is not deluding us when He says He will keep us safe in this world and on into the next ... these are not delusions, they are the truth. When we build our lives on that truth, things happen right for us.

How Do We Live in Reality, Avoiding Deception?

Here are some simple guidelines for living a life free from deception:

1. Don't jump to the wrong conclusions
James 1:19–21 says,

"So then, my beloved brethren, let every man be swift to hear, slow to speak, slow to wrath; for the wrath of man does not produce the righteousness of God. Therefore lay aside all filthiness and overflow of wickedness, and receive with meekness the implanted word, which is able to save your souls."

Being fallible human beings we are prone to jump to wrong conclusions and this leads us to have wrong perceptions about things a lot of the time. We come across a situation that we misunderstand, jump to the wrong conclusion, and the result is we get upset and angry and look for someone to blame. James wisely instructs us that we should not be swift to arrive at such judgments because we only have a limited view of life; we can only see one small piece at a time, only God has the full picture. James says, "Don't be hasty or you will end up believing the wrong thing."

The comedian, Billy Connolly, once starred in a film called *The Man Who Sued God*. In it he was an ex-lawyer who made a claim on his insurance company when his boat was struck by lightning, only to be told they wouldn't pay out because they said it was "an act of God". So he ended up in court trying to prove his case and God got blamed for all kinds of things. In the same way, we can often think that God has caused stuff to happen in our lives when He hasn't. We must not be hasty. A wrong conclusion leads to a wrong response and then we are living in deception.

2. Keep looking in the mirror

The Word of God is like a mirror and if we keep looking into it intently we will not fall into deception. James writes,

> *"For if anyone is a hearer of the word and not a doer, he is like a man observing his natural face in a mirror; for he observes himself, goes away, and immediately forgets what kind of man he was. But he who looks into the perfect law of liberty and continues in it, and is not a forgetful hearer but a doer of the work, this one will be blessed in what he does."*
>
> (JAMES 1:23–25)

We need a "mirror" to keep us on track. I don't have any hard statistics to back up this claim, but my instinct is that women spend a lot more time in front of the mirror than men do! I can always tell when my wife has borrowed my car because my sun visor will be down and the little slide will have been pulled back to reveal the mirror behind it.

We look in the mirror to check that we look OK. James says the Word of God is like a mirror because it tells us where things are at and what we look like. We seem to easily forget who we are in Christ and the mirror of the Word reminds us; it shows us a true reflection of ourselves. When I look into the Word and examine my own reflection I see a man who needs God, a man on a journey who is still growing in Christ. God uses the mirror to remind me that I still need a Saviour.

The Bible tells us many wonderful truths about who we are in Christ, but it also points out where we still need to be fixed. It says it like it is. One of the things I love about the Bible is that even when it talks about heroes like David, it paints a totally honest picture of what he was like. There was a moment when he was an adulterer and a murderer as well as a worshipping warrior. We find these people everywhere in Scripture with their imperfections, but God picks them up and uses them nonetheless. God does amazing things through imperfect ordinary people.

3. Follow the biblical model for your life

Most of us will, from time to time, flick through a magazine looking at the pictures and think, "That looks nice, I wonder if that hairdo would suit me?" or "That's a nice shirt, I wonder if I should wear mine hanging out instead of tucked in?" etc. Whether we realise it or not, we are looking for a model, a pattern we can copy. We see things that appeal to us and replicate them in ourselves. In the same way the Bible provides the perfect pattern for us to follow. James teaches us that not only is the Word of God a mirror that tells us where we are at, it shows us a model of what we can become, revealing the potential of a life in full cooperation with the Holy Spirit.

James talks about the "perfect law of liberty" and says that when we look into it, it makes us realise our potential. It helps us see who we are now, who we would become if we lived to follow every sinful passion and desire that comes to us, and who we can become if we live in obedience to Christ.

God wants us to look into this law of liberty because it sets us free. It tells us that we are valuable, worthwhile, that

Jesus died for us and we are not just amoebas that got lucky! God created us for a purpose and He is with us and will never forsake us.

Jesus said, *"I am the vine; you are the branches. If a man remains in me and I in him, he will bear much fruit; apart from me you can do nothing"* (John 15:5 NIV). One of the great secrets to living free from deception is simply to remain plugged in to God, connected to Jesus. As we keep ourselves aligned with Him we can see a whole new lifestyle develop for us, one based on truth, passion and the power of God's Word and His Spirit.

4. Align yourself to the PAPI lights!

PAPI lights (Precision Approach Path Indicators) are the lights located next to airport runways that help pilots to determine an appropriate approach path when landing. Pilots activate the lights themselves by clicking their microphone on at a particular frequency and the lights stay on for fifteen minutes to help them land. The lights are grouped in fours. When the pilot comes in he wants to see all four red lights at the end of the runway. If he only sees two on the left or two on the right, something is wrong. Two lights on the right mean his aircraft is too high and could overshoot the runway. Two on the left mean his aircraft is too low and could hit the ground before it hits the runway. If the pilot sees all four PAPI lights lit, he knows he's on course.

In his epistle, James lays out the PAPI lights clearly for us and gives us a simple way for us to check that we are still on course. There are two things we need to watch:

1. **Our words**. *"If anyone among you thinks he is religious, and does not bridle his tongue but deceives his own heart, this one's religion is useless"* (James 1:26). We need to make sure that what we say is right, accurate and in line with the Word of God, not negative or critical. Speak words of life.

2. **Our actions**. Faith without works, James says, is dead. He goes further and says that if we have no compassion in our lives to help and touch others, making a difference to them, then our religion is already deceived.

We cannot claim to be living a great Christian life if we have no time for social action and are not active in our community in some way. As the Church we need to impact our communities, touch our youth, be an influence for good in the arts, media, political and business communities. If we are not reaching out to others and putting our lives on the line, then we're already deceived. If we know it all, but are not living in it, it just doesn't work. But if we keep our attention focused intently on these two guiding lights, we will stay on track and not fall into deception. We cannot sub-contract our responsibility to help the helpless. I can give to good causes, but I must also often, frequently give myself to someone. Sending the cash is not enough.

5. Trust the Word of God

James writes, "... *receive with meekness the implanted word*" (James 1:21). We need to hear the Word of God, but we also need to receive it and allow it to be implanted in our hearts so that it becomes a part of our lives. Let the Word of God govern the rhythm of your life and trust it implicitly. The Bible is not just a book, but the living, active, powerful Word of God that has the ability to work in us and transform us from the inside out. God reveals and applies His truth to us as we read and it changes us.

If we trust in the Word of God it can and will have a dramatic effect on us. I was deeply impacted when reading the story of Brother Yun in the book *The Heavenly Man*. Yun played a critical role in the Chinese church, leading millions to faith in Christ.

He became a Christian himself at the age of sixteen. His

father was suffering from asthma, which eventually developed into lung cancer. The cancer spread to his stomach and it was diagnosed that he would soon die. His father was very superstitious and asked some neighbours to fetch a local Daoist priest to come and cast the demons out of him, because he thought that demons were causing the sickness. He parted with all of his money and possessions in the hope of receiving his healing, but of course, he was deceived by a lie.

However, one night after meeting Jesus in a vision, Yun's mother became a Christian and through prayer Yun's father was restored to health. The whole family became Christians. At that time, Bibles were extremely scarce in China and very hard to find, but Yun became desperate to own his own copy of the Word of God. I reproduce a small part of his story here, because it is so inspiring and should cause us to cherish the gift we have in being able to freely read God's Word:

> "I said to my mother, 'Who is this Jesus that we are now believing in?' 'Oh,' she said, 'He's the Son of God who died on the cross taking away our sins and sicknesses. All His teachings are recorded in the Bible.' I asked her, 'Are there any words of Jesus left that I could read for myself?' She replied, 'No, all His words are gone. There's nothing left.' This was during the cultural revolution in the 70s and early 80s. Not one Bible could be found in the land.
>
> From that day on I so much wanted a Bible, just a copy, just a bit of it. I asked my mother and fellow Christians what a Bible looked like, but no one knew. None of them had ever seen one. One person had seen some hand-copied scripture portions and song sheets, but nobody had ever seen a whole Bible. Only a few old believers could recollect seeing a Bible and describe to us what it looked like.

I was so hungry. I nagged my mother, I nagged my father, I nagged anybody who would listen. Then my mother said, 'Well listen. A long way away in a village several days away there's an old pastor. We heard he had a Bible.'

Yun then tells how we journeyed to see this pastor, but he would not show him a Bible. Instead he told Yun to go away and pray for one. He says that he prayed like he had never prayed before, day in and day out, for a whole month but no Bible appeared. He returned to see the pastor again, to be told this time that he should fast and pray with many tears. He did that for several months until one night he received a vision in which he met two men. One said to him, "Are you hungry?" "Oh yes," he replied. The man produced a red box and gave it to Yun. Inside was some bread.

That same day there was a knock on the door of the family home. Because Christians were suffering intense persecution, everyone was afraid to answer the door. Yun writes,

"I went to the door afraid to open it and I said, 'Who's there?' A voice replied and said, 'Are you hungry? I said, 'Yes.' The voice said, 'Are you looking for bread?' I said, 'I am.' 'I have bread for you.' The door opened and standing there were the two men I had seen in the vision. They handed me a red box. They said, 'Several days ago a man in our village, and we live many miles from here, had a vision. He had a Bible that he had buried twenty-five years ago in a red box. God woke him and said, "Dig it up. Send it to this address and give it to this boy."

The two men gave me the red box. I opened it and there was my very own Bible.

The men disappeared. I clutched my new Bible to my heart. I fell down on my knees outside the door. I thanked God again and again. I promised Jesus that from that moment onwards I would devour His Word, I would value every word and every statement – every sentence. I would build my entire life for it, from it."

Today multi-millions in China have come to know Jesus because of the Word of God. As we navigate through life the Word must be our compass. We need to let it dwell in us richly. Let's live by it.

It's in here we find faith, and faith makes us champions. Faith takes us through doubt and beyond it. We can empathise with John Bunyon who said, "Doubt has as many lives as a cat." With the Word and faith and faith and the Word we will live well.

6. Walk in humility

The pastor I spoke of earlier who illegally married people was challenged by other pastors who loved him enough to tell him he was wrong and breaking the law. He replied that being a servant of God and a representative of Heaven he did not need man's paper to make his practice right. That's called deception, induced by arrogance. The truth is, this man was relatively successful. The church grew, the buildings came and the money flowed.

Dr Martyn Lloyd-Jones said, "The worst thing a man can do is have success before he is ready." Many men have come through their failures, not so many can handle their successes. Just because you have big churches or big faith does not make you right!

In the book *From Good to Great*, the authors study the biggest, best and most successful companies in the world. The one hallmark they found in all of the greatest leaders was humility. Not an "I am hopeless" mentality, but an outlook that said, "I always need to learn and there is the possibility I could be wrong!" Further, they were not interested in trying to keep up appearances – an activity that so often results in limited friendships and leaves us high and dry on a pedestal from which we will eventually fall. Humility allows others to input into us, to correct us and to get close enough to really see what's going on. We can't be that way with everyone – that would be foolish and we would very soon be hurt. But we need other people, real friends who are prepared to say to us, "That doesn't sound right . . . " to help us avoid walking in deception.

> **"The patronage of the great is nothing
> to the favour of the Lord.
> Self-reliance is very well,
> but the Lord's blessing is infinitely more
> than the fruit of talent, genius or tact."**
> (C.H. Spurgeon)

CHAPTER 4

OVERCOMING
A NEGATIVE
LIFESTYLE

*"When we are in the right state of heart
faith costs no effort."*
(C.H. Spurgeon)

Once I saw the pop star Lionel Ritchie interviewed on Michael Parkinson's chat show. Parkinson asked him, "Do you ever get scared before you go on stage?" Ritchie replied, "I used to when I was starting out, but I don't any more. The stage is easy. On the stage all our words are rehearsed and prepared. Everybody knows where they're supposed to be standing, every technician knows what they're going to do

73

next, every musician has got his music prepared. We've gone through it a hundred times! So the stage is easy. It's life that's hard." He then began to talk about the divorce he'd been through, the struggles he'd had in raising his kids, the questions they ask him that he can't answer, and so on. He said, "It's in the spontaneity of life that I sometimes find I don't know how to live!"

James' epistle was written to answer that very question – to help us find out how to live life when and as it happens. In this chapter we will look at what he has to say about staying clear of a negative lifestyle and the single most important aspect of this will be the control we have or don't have over our tongues. We read,

> *"Let not many of you become teachers, my brethren, knowing that as such we will incur a stricter judgment. For we all stumble in many ways. If anyone does not stumble in what he says, he is a perfect man, able to bridle the whole body as well. Now if we put the bits into the horses' mouths so that they will obey us, we direct their entire body as well. Look at the ships also, though they are so great and are driven by strong winds, are still directed by a very small rudder wherever the inclination of the pilot desires. So also the tongue is a small part of the body, and yet it boasts of great things. See how great a forest is set aflame by such a small fire! And the tongue is a fire, the very world of iniquity; the tongue is set among our members as that which defiles the entire body, and sets on fire the course of our life, and is set on fire by hell. For every species of beasts and birds, of reptiles and creatures of the sea, is tamed and has been tamed by the human race. But no one can tame the tongue; it is a restless evil and full of deadly poison. With it we bless our Lord and Father, and with it we curse men, who have been made in the likeness of God; from the same mouth come both blessing and cursing. My brethren, these things ought not to be this way. Does a fountain send out from the same opening both fresh and bitter water? Can a fig tree, my*

brethren, produce olives, or a vine produce figs? Nor can salt
water produce fresh."

(JAMES 3:1–12 NASB)

Before I entered into full-time ministry as a pastor I was in
the world of business. Then, as now, I was passionate about
developing strong leaders. Leaders make things happen.
When leadership is strong, whether it's in the commercial
world or inside the Church, everyone prospers.

Over the years I've read perhaps hundreds of books on
leadership that have focused on aspects such as management,
the power of a positive mental attitude, vision, goal-setting,
even controlling our emotions, but I have never once found a
book written by a business person that focuses on the tongue
and how we speak. Yet, according to James, this is the biggest
issue. The tongue is our interface with life. We connect and
communicate with each other by using it. We can build
people up or cut them into pieces with it. It's the only way
you know what's going on inside me – by what I tell you.
Jesus told us the hidden things of the heart come right out
of the mouth. I have been amazed how often there is a
correlation between what you say and what you get. You can
see this even in a sports interview when a reporter interviews
a team coach. Listen to what he says before a game and then
watch for the result. If he speaks doubt, "Oh, it's going to be
a tough one," then the team nearly always gets what they say!
Do your own survey and see for yourself.

If we want to learn how to "do life" successfully, therefore, we have to begin with our tongue.

James emphasises over and over again the power our
words have and the influence our tongues have on our lives.
There are three main points he brings out and these will
determine whether we live negative lifestyles or positive,
life-affirming ones. The tongue has,

- The power to destroy
- The power to direct
- The power to deliver

THE TONGUE HAS THE POWER TO DESTROY

In 1899 four newspaper reporters from Denver, Colorado, sat down together on a Saturday night in the Denver railway depot. They were Al Stevens, Jack Tourney, John Lewis and Hal Wilshire and they represented the four Denver newspapers: *The Post*, *The Times*, *The Republican* and *Rocky Mountain News*.

Each of these newspapers had sent its respective reporter to dig up a story. It was Saturday night and the Sunday papers were due, so they badly needed something! The reporters were waiting at the railway station hoping some visiting celebrity would roll into town, they'd do an interview and they would have their story for the following day.

Unfortunately, it was a quiet evening and no one arrived. They commiserated together and then Al said, "I'm going to make up a story. I'm going to write anything and hand it in." Someone else suggested that they should all walk over to the Oxford Hotel, have a beer and *each* make up a story. They did this, but then Jack said that though he liked Al's idea about faking a story, if they had four different fake stories no one would believe them. What they should do is make up one fake story and publish it in all four newspapers!

They had another round of beers and decided to get to work. What phoney story could they write that wouldn't be so easy to check? Maybe one that discusses foreign nations or foreign angles was the reply. "Hey, China's distant enough," someone said. "Why don't we write about China?"

John leaned forward, pulling his comrades closer, and said, "Try this one: we'll write that a group of American engineers has stopped over in Denver and they're on their way to China to pull down the Great Wall of China. The Chinese Government is making plans to demolish the Great Wall and our engineers are bidding for the job!"

Hal was sceptical: "Why would the Chinese want to destroy the Great Wall of China. It's been there thousands of years ... " John thought for a moment and then said, "I know, it's an ancient boundary and we want to destroy it, so the Chinese say, to symbolise international goodwill and to welcome foreign trade."

"Great idea! Let's have another round of beers."

By 11.00pm the four reporters had worked out the story and the next day all four newspapers printed it. In fact, it began to spread. The headline read:

"GREAT CHINESE WALL DOOMED! PEKING SEEKS WORLD TRADE!"

The story began to travel so fast that, over the next few weeks, virtually all the US papers picked it up and began to publish it. Then the European papers began to publish it as well and the whole world was talking about it. John Lewis noticed that a large Eastern US newspaper had picked up the story and even included information not in the original story with supposed quotes from a Chinese mandarin confirming it! Although the story underwent different versions, the essence remained: the United States was sending an expedition to tear down the Great Wall of China. Years later, the last surviving reporter of the hoax, Hal Wilshire, confessed the secret.

The publication of the article coincided with a terrible period of unrest in China. A peasant-based group called the Boxer Movement had begun the year before and rapidly gained in numbers. The Boxers were anti-foreign and anti-imperialist. They attacked foreigners who had come to the land to build railroads, as well as Christians who they blamed for the increasing foreign domination of China. In the June of 1900 the Boxers invaded Beijing and murdered 230 non-Chinese. The movement had escalated into a full-blown uprising which became known as the Boxer Rebellion. During the uprising, tens of thousands of Chinese Christians were slaughtered.

An urban legend, begun in 1939 by Denver-based song-writer Harry Lee Wilber, suggested that the 1899 hoax article had in fact ignited the Boxer Rebellion. Nothing in the history books corroborates this view, and it would be very hard to prove the link. But the article, carried by so many Western news publications, cannot have helped matters in any sense.

Make no mistake: the words we use can affect lives all around us. During the Second World War posters warning against disclosing secrets read "Words Cost Lives."

James rightly says that the tongue has the power to destroy. In verse 8 he says, *"No one can tame the tongue! It is a restless evil and full of deadly poison!"* (NASB).

John Calvin, the great theological Reformer, said,

"Other vices in our lives are often corrected by age or the process of time. Eventually we get on top of them or we grow out of them. They drop off from our lives. But from the earliest to the last the tongue remains."

We are prone to misuse our tongues in a variety of destructive ways. We use our tongues to destroy by gossiping, talking about others in a derogatory way behind their backs. We use our tongues to destroy when we flatter, saying one thing to a person's face – "Oh, you're a great fellow. What you're doing is fantastic!" – and then shooting them down later. The tongue has the power to destroy by innuendo, when we say things that are not exactly a lie, but not exactly the truth. All that we say has an effect on the lives of those around us.

About 150 years ago there was a ship's captain who wrote up his log every day. One of the ship's mates was constantly drunk so the captain wrote, "The ship's mate is drunk again." The captain, being tired, took rest and the mate took responsibility for the ship. He read the log and was really upset that the captain had been recording his drunkenness, so he opened the book and wrote down, "The captain is sober today." It was true, because the captain was sober every day, but when you read it in that way the implication was that something questionable was going on!

James, because he is passionate about life and the wellbeing of the Church, urges us, "Listen! Don't use your tongues to destroy!" In fact, he goes further than this and tells us that the tongue is the pipeline from hell to earth! *"... the tongue is a fire, the very world of iniquity"* (v. 6). What he means by this is that the insidious, devious, discouraging, awful, negative world of Satan finds its way into our world by no other means than our tongues. James was precise in his use of language. The word he used for "world" was *cosmos*, which in the Bible usually means "a way of government that is anti-God".

Debilitating emotions such as anger, bitterness, hatred and jealousy don't gain entrance into our personal lives or into the Church because some demon comes knocking on our door. These influences come through the pipeline of our tongue! Man has learned how to conquer or tame many things in this world, but who, James asks, can rule the tongue? So we need to be very careful.

On 8 October, 1871, a fire broke out in a barn at 137 DeKoven Street which swept across the City of Chicago and became known as the Great Chicago Fire. The fire killed hundreds of people and destroyed four square miles of the city. 17,500 buildings were razed to the ground, some $222 million worth – a third of the entire city's valuation –

and of the 300,000 population about 90,000 were left homeless as a result.

James warns us, "Make no mistake, your words can start fires that cannot be put out." Just like the Chicago blaze that firemen struggled to put out, our words can inflame and set ablaze situations and it is almost impossible to reverse the damage. We have to get a grip on our tongues!

When I was a child we had a rhyme,

> "Sticks and stones can break my bones, but names will never hurt me."

Well, the bruises heal and the bones mend, but damage done by words goes deep inside a person. It is there until they die unless the impact of those words is dealt with.

THE TONGUE HAS THE POWER TO DIRECT

In the same way that a great ship is steered by a little rudder or a powerful horse can be steered by the bit in its mouth, if we can get a grip on the way we speak we can steer our lives into incredible destinies.

Proverbs 18:21 tells us,

> *"Death and life are in the power of the tongue,*
> *And those who love it will eat its fruit."*
>
> (NASB)

The tongue has the power to be destructive, but it also has the power to impart life. Throughout his epistle James teaches his readers that faith is not just about what you think in your heart, it is about what you do with your life. It's not just an emotional experience, it is based on actions too. The same is true of our words, James says. Faith operates in our lives by the words we speak.

In James 3:6 he says,

*"... the tongue is set among our members as that which defiles the entire body, and sets on fire **the course of our life** ... "*
(emphasis added)

James uses the phrase "the course of our life". Since the tongue holds the power of both death and life, we can draw from this that negative, destructive speech will affect the entire course of our lives for the worse, but conversely, positive faith-filled speech will affect the course of our lives for the better.

The Greek words used to create this short phrase are fascinating and insightful. The Greek word for "course" is the same word as for "wheel" and the word for "life" is the same word that means "genesis". Translated literally then, the phrase *"the course of our life"* becomes *"the wheel of our genesis"*. It carries the sense that the words we speak create a *"wheel of genesis"* or "creation" for us. The words we speak have creative power which put in motion our destiny.

If you think that's stretching the analogy too far, one needs only to look at the account of creation itself. We see that when God created the planet He did it with words. Time again the Bible tells us, "And God said ... and God said ... "

I am intrigued by the scientific "string theory" that many notable scientists hold to. Simply put, it argues that a sound wave is the smallest particle in the universe. As they cannot yet see something that small, the theory remains unproven. But one thing is for sure, words make more than sound waves – they make worlds, my world, your world and the world around us.

I've been in ministry many years and during that time I've sat down with countless people in counselling situations. So often people come for help because of issues in their lives related to words – usually things people have said to them that have deeply wounded them. Words spoken in anger or with malice endure. I often counsel people who are broken because years and years ago someone said to them, "You're hopeless ... I never really wanted you ... you were a mistake ... you're such a pain..." etc. Words were spoken over them that created an inner world of negativity, of insecurity, of zero self-worth, and now, years later, they need counselling and help because those words created a world.

We need to understand that the words we speak, whether they be about our marriage, our business, our kids, our health, or any other situation, always create something. They steer our lives and give them direction, set them on a particular course.

Some people have a habit of speaking their mind without thinking through what they are about to say, blurting out the first thing that comes into their head. This is a bad habit because the devil likes to infiltrate our minds and plant unwholesome, unhelpful ideas there. He likes to undermine us by saying things like, "There's no future for you ... you're too old, you're past it ... you're too young and inexperienced ... you haven't got what it takes, you'll never make it ... this is not going to work out ... the experts have said ..." etc.

The worst thing you can do with those thoughts is verbalise them. Speaking them out actually reinforces them, because you are applying the creative power of the tongue to them. If you refuse to speak out those negative thoughts about yourself (which, when compared to the truth of God's Word about you are utter lies), even though they may persist, they will die unborn. They will have no power over you unless you choose to give birth to them through speech. We are made in God's image and if God can create a world with His words, we can move the "wheel of our life" with our own words. If we will discipline our tongues and work on improving the quality of our speech then we will create a different world for ourselves.

Think for a moment and ask yourself, "What kind of world am I creating with my words?" Fathers and mothers, what kind of world are you creating in your home? Church leaders, what kind of world are you creating in your church? Teachers, what are you saying over your class? The truth is we are all too often unleashing hell itself. If parents row and say hurtful things to one another, it creates insecurity in their kids. If leaders, whether in the Church or in business, go around saying, "I don't know what I'm going to do!" or "these people are hopeless" it creates uncertainty and insecurity. It makes people wonder if there will be a job there for them tomorrow, or if they even want the job that's there for them tomorrow. If you are the boss, people are looking to you. Your words are very important!

> **"A sharp tongue often cuts its own throat."**
> (Jim Scancerelli)

Moses learnt this. When he was leading the people across the Red Sea, the people were crying out, "We want to go back!" Moses just said to them, "Peace, be still," despite the fact that in his heart he was crying out to God. Read the story, for it tells us that in his heart Moses was yelling out to God, but he refused to speak out his fear. Sometimes our prayers need to be "inner" prayers between us and God, if praying them out would have a negative effect on others or on our situation.

Here is something else important: only God is omniscient and knows everything, the devil does not. God knows what's going on in your heart because His Spirit searches it out, but the devil doesn't know. The only way the devil gets to know what's going on inside of you is when you speak it out. Then he can say, "Ha, he's worried, let's hike up the pressure. He's anxious. He's panicking. Great! He's going to make a bad decision now! He's in unbelief. He's losing his faith. Just a bit more shaking and he'll let go of his dreams and hopes."

So, it is important to speak out the positive and not the negative. Using our tongues positively will guide us into a positive, faith-filled future. As Proverbs 10:11 reminds us,

"The mouth of the righteous is a fountain of life."

(NASB)

In case anyone thinks this is sounding like "head-in-the-sand" positive confession type of faith that has no basis in reality, we have to be real, but at the same time align ourselves with the truth of the Word of God. Once in our church, a lady responded to an altar call for healing. She stood in line as we prayed for those who were sick and when it was her turn I asked her, "What's wrong with you?" She replied, "There's nothing wrong with me." I said, "But this is a healing line, we're praying for the sick. Only sick people need to stand here." She responded, "Well, I have the symptoms of the flu, but I haven't got it really. It's not here. It doesn't exist!" She had got confused over the issue of reality and confession. To clarify, let me show you a person who handled this supremely well. We read in Romans chapter 4:

"(as it is written, 'A FATHER OF MANY NATIONS HAVE I MADE YOU') in the presence of Him whom he believed, even God, who gives life to the dead and calls into being that which does not exist. In hope against hope he believed, so that he might become a father of many nations according to that which had been spoken, 'SO SHALL YOUR DESCENDANTS BE.' Without becoming weak in faith he contemplated his own

body, now as good as dead since he was about a hundred years old, and the deadness of Sarah's womb; yet, with respect to the promise of God, he did not waver in unbelief but grew strong in faith, giving glory to God, and being fully assured that what God had promised, He was able also to perform."

(ROMANS 4:17–21 NASB)

Paul is writing, of course, about Abraham, the man to whom in his old age God said, "You're going to have a child." Abraham was astonished by this news. Perhaps he looked at himself in the mirror and thought, "You're past it!" Then he looked at his wife, Sarah, and thought, "She's past it too!" In fact, the Bible says he considered his body, "as good as dead". The important thing is, Abraham didn't start making crazy proclamations of faith like, "Hey, I'm not past it at all, I'm still young and vibrant!" He acknowledged the reality of the situation, but professed his confidence in God. He said, in effect, "My body is as good as dead, but God isn't!"

See that there is often a difference between facts and truth. Abraham was old – fact! But God was able and willing – truth! Our focus should always be on what God has said about a particular situation, not on the situation itself. We may be in difficulty, facing unemployment or sickness, something we hadn't bargained for, but we can confess with absolute certainty, "God has said He will never leave me or forsake me ... all things are possible for those who believe." We may recall a promise that God specifically gave us in the past and keep holding fast to it. No matter how much pressure comes upon us, we must never give up the ground we have already taken spiritually.

In verse 17 of Romans 4 we read that God is the One, *"... who gives life to the dead and calls into being that which does not exist."* Remember when Jesus raised Lazarus from the dead, He called out, "Lazarus! Come forth!"? The way that God continually breaks into our lives is by calling us with a word.

He calls to us, "Come on!" and when we respond to His word, life enters our very being. If you are waiting for divine intervention in some situation in your life, listen for a word from God, because He wants to speak into your situation a specific word for that problem. God can call into being things which "are not" and completely reverse a person's circumstances. Our response needs to be the same as Abraham's was: "I believe You, God. I know You are able. I trust You." This is the right kind of faith proclamation.

THE TONGUE HAS THE POWER TO COMPLETELY DELIVER

Proverbs 12:18 tells us that, *"the tongue of the wise brings healing"* (NASB). Being able to control one's tongue is a sign of spiritual maturity, but it is more than that. Controlling the tongue is *the means by which we become mature*. Mastering our tongues is a incredible method of self-deliverance – it will save us from a whole heap of trouble!

If we learn to use our tongues positively, it will result in keeping us on course to reach our destiny in Christ. Below I have listed six ways, each beginning with a "p", in which we can use our words positively:

1. Prepare your lips
Thinking before we speak is something that few people have completely mastered. It is just too easy to react impulsively to people or situations. But we need to develop the art of preparing our lips, considering our words before we use them. The great prophet Isaiah, when he encountered the awesome presence of God in the temple, was forced to admit, "God, I'm undone. I'm a man of unclean lips..." God instructed an angel to touch Isaiah's lips with a burning coal from the altar and he was cleansed. God cauterized his lips. Daily we need to prepare our lips. We need to cauterize

the negativity, seal up the things that are unwholesome, and apply the balm of the Word of God.

2. Protect your church
Rick Warren, in his book *The Purpose-Driven Life*, says this:

> "It is your job to protect the unity of the Church. Unity of the Church is so important that the New Testament gives more attention to it than either heaven or hell. God deeply desires that we experience oneness and harmony with each other. Unity is the soul of fellowship. Destroy it and you rip the heart out of the body. It's the essence, the core, of how God intends for us to experience life together in His Church. Our supreme model for unity is the Trinity – Father, Son and Holy Spirit – completely unified."

There is nothing worse than division and backbiting in a church. It causes disunity and undermines the work of God. We need to protect our churches by guarding our speech as we fellowship with one another. This is not just for leaders, but for everyone. The Enemy would love to destroy your church and mine any way he can. One of the ways in which he consistently works is by spreading malicious rumours and gossip, causing erosion to spread from within. Whenever we hear whispering beginning amongst fellow church members, we need to be brave enough to address it and say, "We shouldn't be talking like this." Speak up and protect the unity of your church.

3. Promote your brother
We should use our lips to promote one another, rather than criticize one another – promotion, that is, in the sense of encouraging and lifting each other up, not in the sense of empty flattery. Telling someone, "Hey, you did great" or

"What you shared really spoke to me" or "You're so faithful in serving the church" goes a long way and everyone, without exception, needs affirmation and encouragement.

4. Praise God

The effect that praising God can have in our lives has to be experienced to be fully appreciated. Learning to say, "Thank You, Lord," more often than we say, "Why me, Lord?" can have a powerful effect on our wellbeing and perspective on life.

Paul and Silas were in the deepest prison at the darkest hour. They had just taken a beating and were not exactly on top of their world. But in it all they praised God and then praised Him some more by singing hymns. Without warning the entire prison was shaken, the door burst open and their shackles were loosed. Praise not only set them free, it set the whole community free.

> **"God sits down on the praises of His people."**

And when He sits down everything else just has to move over!

Praise is so often a sacrifice. We may not feel like praising, we have to force it through unwilling lips. Often we just don't feel like it, but we need to do it anyway.

It is a well known fact that we tend to gravitate towards that on which our attention is focused. So we need to focus on something positive and make that our confession, praising God instead of focusing on our problems. Praise is a choice, it's not a feeling or an emotion. Whatever happens to us we can choose to praise God regardless.

> **"A praising person conquers pressures!"**

5. Pray

The Bible says we should offer prayers up at every opportunity and on every occasion. We don't need seek out some holy place to pray, we can just do it wherever we are and whatever we're doing. The most positive use of our tongues is to speak out words of prayer. The moment we begin pray Jesus says that the Father responds, if we ask in His name. Here's a good prayer prayed by David:

> *"Let the words of my mouth and the meditation of my heart*
> *Be acceptable in Your sight,*
> *O Lord..."*

(PSALM 19:14)

6. Profess your confession

Did you know you can't get saved with out saying so! We read in Romans 10:9,

> *"If you confess with your mouth Jesus as Lord, and believe in your heart that God raised Him from the dead, you will be saved."*

(NASB)

This is the ultimate use of our tongues – to confess and profess our faith in Jesus Christ as our Lord and Saviour. What better way is there to use our words? So let's guard our mouths and make sure that we don't slip into a negative lifestyle, but fill our lives with positive, faith-filled confessions of truth that will set us on course to fulfil our destiny.

The Christian faith starts the way it is meant to go on! If we come to God by a confession of our mouths then we will walk with Him in the same way. The writer of Hebrews urges us to, *"hold fast the confession of* [your] *hope without wavering"* (Hebrews 10:23).

Find ways to speak God's Word into your world. Speak it over your home, your famiy, your finances, work, church and community. Look around your world and with un-wavering hope bring into being the world God has painted in your heart, the world you can see on the canvas of your imagination. God always creates twice, first in you and then through you.

> **"Dreams are not bound to the dream world."**
> (Watanabe, President of Toyota)

CHAPTER 5

OVERCOMING THE STRIFE IN YOUR LIFE

*"We must learn to live together like brothers
or perish together like fools."*
(Martin Luther King Jr)

Each year more and more new words enter our vocabulary or have their meanings extended. "Mouse" and "virus" are typical examples of words that now have more than one meaning. But how about this?

During the Second World War a number of new words and phrases were coined. One such word was "Snafu". Military personnel used this abbreviation in their communications when things had gone wrong with their plans. It stood for "Situation normal: all fouled up". In more recent times, during the Gulf War, soldiers invented a new version: "Fubb", which means "Fouled up beyond belief"!

Is your life *fubbed*?

All too often this is where we are. Just like someone said,

"The trouble with me is that I am in tune with Chaos."

If we examine our personal lives, our home life, our work, or our relationships in close detail, we may find that the diagnosis is *fubbed*! Similarly, if we take an inventory of the life of many churches they would also be *fubbed*. We look and we find judgmental attitudes, criticism, dissension, arguments, the breakdown of relationships and an assault on leadership. So often things are not the way they are meant to be.

I had one woman leave one of our churches shouting, "Just look at it!" pointing at the folks who stood at the church door smoking their last cigarette before they came in. Despite pointing out that this was really the smallest of the issues these particular people faced and far more serious issues were being dealt with, she still failed to see the "plank" the size of a railway sleeper sticking out of her own eye! Instead of dealing with her own pharisaical attitude she was busy knocking everyone else over with it. There is one word we can use to describe all of this: *strife*.

We read in chapter 3 of his epistle James gives us some keys to overcoming strife in our life:

"Who among you is wise and understanding? Let him show by his good behaviour his deeds in the gentleness of wisdom. But if you have bitter jealousy and selfish ambition in your heart, do not be arrogant and so lie against the truth. This wisdom is not that which comes down from above, but is earthly, natural, demonic.

For where jealousy and selfish ambition exist, there is disorder and every evil thing. But the wisdom from above is first pure, then peaceable, gentle, reasonable, full of mercy and good fruits, unwavering, without hypocrisy. And the seed whose fruit is righteousness is sown in peace by those who make peace."

(JAMES 3:13–18 NASB)

James was passionate to build the Church into a winning team. He wanted to see the Church thrive and succeed wherever God planted it, because he realised that the Church was Jesus' big idea, and there is nothing as exciting as when a big idea's moment has arrived. The Church was not put on the earth simply for the comfort of Christians, but to advance God's kingdom, to take ground, to make a difference. Military generals will tell you that it takes seven times more fire power to advance than to hold ground. This is James' fire power coming into action, his God-given bullets made for shooting down the enemy.

James acknowledged that there were things in the Church that should not be there, issues that affected the Church of his day, just as they affect the Church of ours. He recognised that there existed difficulties and strife that, if not dealt with, would impede the Church from moving forward and rob it of its power. All too often the strife leaves people thinking like this,

"I would believe in their salvation if they looked a little bit more like they were saved."

(Friedrich Nietzsche, atheist philosopher)

We can all do without strife in our lives, whether it is personal or corporate, so we need to follow James' advice to counteract it. James imparts godly wisdom. First of all, he says, we must have an accurate diagnosis of the problem.

DIAGNOSIS

When attempting to address any problem in life, before action can be taken there has to be an accurate diagnosis. If we go to see an optician because we are having trouble with our eyes, we don't expect him to say, "Yes, I can see you're having difficulty seeing, here, take my glasses. I've worn them for fifteen years and they've done me the world of good!" In fact, if we put his glasses on it could well make things worse, since they are his glasses, not ours. Such a situation would be ridiculous. Instead, we need a careful diagnosis of our condition and to apply an appropriate remedy.

Similarly, we live in a world surrounded by family, friends and work colleagues, most of whom truly want to help us. But so often we find that when we have a problem, all the people around us try to take off their "glasses" and put them on us: "Here, this worked for me so it will work for you." The fact is, without a correct diagnosis and a proper source for a solution we will never have a workable answer.

James' diagnosis regarding strife is this: the condition of many people's lives is **fubbed** because they are operating with the wrong kind of wisdom. In fact, the Bible says it's not wisdom at all but utter foolishness. A simple definition of wisdom is: the ability to make the right response to a given situation. In most situations we will go with our natural reaction, and nine times out of ten that will be wrong. We should look instead for *response-ability* – knowing what is the right thing to do when faced with a decision or dilemma and choosing to do it. We can only do this by accessing God's wisdom.

> "The lowest level of knowledge is assumption.
> Above that we have information,
> then comes understanding, over and above this
> is wisdom which results in the highest form of
> knowledge – a life that is worth living."

I recently came across the following story that demonstrates the folly of human wisdom:

In 1845, Royal Navy Rear-Admiral Sir John Franklin and 134 specially chosen officers and men left England to find the North West Passage. They sailed in two three-masted ships, one called *The Erebus*, which means "dark place" and the other called *The Terror*. Not exactly a good start, was it?

Each ship was equipped with an auxiliary steam engine and could hold an additional twelve-day supply of coal, should steam power be needed for the times when, during the anticipated two to three year voyage, the winds would fail. However, instead of loading the reserve coal as planned, each ship made room for a 1,200 volume library, an organ, and an elegant dining table with a full place setting for all officers on board that included china, cut glass goblets and sterling silver flatware. In fact, all the officers' silver flatware had their family crests and initials engraved on them.

Furthermore, the only clothing that these sailors took with them on the voyage were their proud English uniforms and great coats of Her Majesty's Navy.

The ships sailed off amidst imperial pomp and glory and were sent off with great celebration. Two months later a couple of British whaling ships, the *Prince of Wales* and the *Enterprise*, met the two ships in Baffin Bay and reports were carried back to England of the expedition's high spirits and positive outlook. But these ships were the last to see them alive.

After some time, search parties were funded by Lady Jane Franklin, the wife of the commander, and the search parties brought back a tragic story. Further information was gathered from Eskimos of the events of the day it all went wrong.

People had seen men pushing a wooden boat across the ice. Others had found the boat. Some had found the bodies of thirty men, fully clothed, with silk cravats, frozen to death in the artic ice. For the next twenty years search parties would recover skeletons from the frozen waste and twelve years later it was learned that Admiral Franklin had died aboard the ship sitting at his table with his cut glass and sterling silver flatware.

The Franklin expedition was a monumental failure by every standard. It was foolishly conceived, foolishly planned, foolishly equipped and foolishly carried out. The expedition itself served absolutely no purpose other than to teach the sailors who followed it to apply the right sort of wisdom when attempting to navigate the North West Passage. Being warm was more important than appearances, and using space for necessary equipment was more important that pianos and silverware.

Well, some would say, we wouldn't do anything as daft these days. But we do all the time. Some people think the right way to get peace in the Middle East is "hit them harder than they hit us". All that produces is perpetual hatred. Then we have the modern attitude of "tolerance". We must be tolerant of everything. Except, of course, of the notion that there is such a thing as absolute truth. We can't tolerate that. If Jesus claimed today as He did then, "I am the way the truth and the life", it would attract just as much of a "take Him away and kill Him" attitude from our modern world as it did when He first proclaimed it.

Then we have scientism – the doctrines of Richard Dawkins and his kind. They argue that the only things you can believe in are those that can be proven by scientific methods. They don't pause to think that such statements themselves cannot be proven by scientific methods, so it's not science they are advocating but scientism, their own form of atheism. I read recently,

> **"The trouble with atheists these days is that they insist on bringing God into everything!"**

Just look at Dawkins, he does it all the time. Why is he so consumed with a God he says he doesn't believe in? There are many things in life we know are a reality, even though we cannot prove them empirically. No one can scientifically prove the truth of my love for my wife, for instance, yet it exists.

Human wisdom would espouse a survival-of-the-fittest doctrine and would perhaps say that logically, you should have as many wives as possible because that will provide the most benefit to the species. That is where the Dawkins-type thought process naturally leads. But God's wisdom says there is a better way, a way of fidelity and commitment, a way that tells us relationships are worth fighting for and the journey we take with others is often more important than the tasks accomplished at the end.

We are constantly being programmed by worldly non-wisdom that seeks to influence our lives from an early age. It comes in many forms, sometimes proclaiming itself loudly and at other times quietly infiltrating our thinking and our value systems. The values of worldly non-wisdom are contrary to godly wisdom. Worldly non-wisdom says that if we want to get anything in life, we have to fight for it; we need to be assertive, to grasp and grab, advance more by using our elbows instead of our knees and, if necessary, steal reputations or step on others in the process. Hardly like Jesus is it?

Once we are programmed with this worldly non-wisdom, we end up living as Christians with pagan values. We bring the non-wisdom way of life with us into the church and home. It manifests whenever people are more concerned about their position and influence than living like Jesus. We can even use our kids to do it. Competing with each other on their successes and hiding their failures; trophy hunting for the next "brag ball". But even if we win this game, we end up feeling awful inside, hating ourselves and the environment we create.

This is not how God intended us to live!

Negative scripting

When James talks about strife he refers to strife in the home, between a husband and wife, between parents and their kids, or strife in the workplace. He speaks of "selfish ambition" which means "canvassing for your opinion to be heard" and carries the sense of a politician who doesn't want to see anyone else's point of view, but loudly promotes his own cause.

Strife is often the cause of "negative scripting", where someone so forcefully and persistently puts across their opinion that any person who has to listen to them is virtually programmed by it. When an actor stands on stage he is required to say what's in his script and the director tells him what to say and when. In the same way, some parents have been the directors of their kids, but not in a positive way. Instead they have given their children negative scripts to act out their lives. Parents can do this with the words they use but also by their actions. This is why we abused people go on to abuse other people and kids who suffer violence at home often end up being violent in school or on the streets. They were given a negative script based on worldly wisdom. Hurt people hurt people!

Kingdom values

When we become a Christian and a part of the kingdom of God, however, we don't just accept a new set of beliefs, we enter a whole new culture, an entirely different way of thinking based on different wisdom.

God's wisdom does not counsel us to fight for what we want and does not even advocate competitiveness. Kingdom values go completely against the grain of the world's thinking. Because of our pre-programming we have a tendency to think that if we don't assert ourselves we will be the doormats of society, plus we will miss out on every opportunity for promotion. But this is not the case in God's kingdom because the Bible tells us it is God Himself who promotes us when the time is right.

James writes, *"And the seed whose fruit is righteousness is sown in peace by those who make peace"* (James 3:18 NASB). What he is saying here is that "fruit", or in other words "success", in life doesn't come by us manufacturing it for ourselves. It comes when we surrender to God and allow Him to work His purposes in us and through us. Jesus promised, *"Seek first the kingdom of God and His righteousness, and all these things shall be added to you"* (Matthew 6:33).

The Bible teaches that God's people are destined to be the head and not the tail, i.e. we are destined to thrive and live in blessing, not be continually oppressed and down-trodden. But we don't get ourselves into that position by fighting how the world fights. All that does is produce strife. We need to ask God to reverse the negative scripting that has taken place in our lives, lay down all our worldly non-wisdom, and plug into God's wisdom for our lives.

DEPOSITS

James has more to say about the way in which godly wisdom – the antidote to strife – functions. He writes,

"But the wisdom from above is first pure, then peaceable, gentle, reasonable, full of mercy and good fruits, unwavering, without hypocrisy."

(JAMES 3:17 NASB)

If we want to live our lives in such a way that they work out as God intended, then we need interact with people and handle our relationships in the way that James describes. I like to think of this as having a deliberate strategy to make "deposits" in the lives of others.

Have you ever been to the bank to make a withdrawal only to discover there are no funds to draw on. It's very simple, we've made too many withdrawals but no deposits! People call it being "in the red". Many of us are in emotional/relational red living and urgently need to make some deposits. We can make deposits in a variety of ways: by affirming our partners or friends, encouraging our kids or our colleagues, or by creating an atmosphere in which it's OK to say if you have a need without being judged.

A while ago I sat down with a family to talk through some difficulties they were having, having had to do it so often with my own. The relationships were strained. I encouraged them to be open with one another and to calmly put forward their points of view. The mother began by saying to her daughter, "Listen, I love you, I do, and I want you to be able to say anything you want to say here. I want you to share your heart. I know we've got some difficulties over your education right now, but I just want you to share."

The daughter said, "OK, Mum. I find school boring. It's dull, irrelevant and I don't want to be there."

Her mother immediately flared up, "See! You just don't appreciate the effort we've put in to get you there! You should shake up your attitude and get stuck in!"

So often what we deposit in others is not what we intended! Maybe this lady reacted so strongly because of her own inbuilt negative scripting. But we all have an opportunity to replace that with positive scripting based on the truth of the Word of God, and to then make positive affirming deposits in others. Whether it's our family, friends, church members, work colleagues, or anyone else, we need to make good deposits in their lives.

The mother, and others like her would be better saying, "OK, let's find a way forward together."

Recently a guy who had attended our church for a little while left and moved elsewhere. He was quite a pleasant person, nice to speak to and often humorous. But just before he left I quickly reviewed all the emails he had sent me over a three-year period and was shocked to discover that out of about twenty-five emails, twenty-three of them were criticising the church, albeit in ever such a nice way: "I just really wanted to point out something to be helpful..." etc. The reality was, twenty-three out twenty-five of his communications to me were not making a positive contribution to my relationship with him. Perhaps, if I had received even just a few that said something positive like, "The worship really blessed me today" or "God really spoke to me through your message", he would have made enough of a deposit into our relationship to make his constructive criticism heard. But when everything coming was negative it was difficult to take any of it on board. Since leaving he has jumped church a few more times. Too many of us only make negative deposits and wonder why we hit a brick wall in our progress.

DENIAL

If we want to avoid strife in our lives then we need to be able to say "no" to some things in life. Matthew 16:24 says,

"Then Jesus said to His disciples, 'If anyone desires to come after Me, let him deny himself, and take up his cross, and follow Me.'"

To live life as God intended means knowing how to deny ourselves. When I last looked I couldn't find a "Teach Yourself Self-Denial" book or even "Denial for Dummies". It contrasts sharply with the worldly non-wisdom of "grab all you can and can all you grab"!

Some people accumulate huge debts because they never say no. They spend compulsively on their credit cards and don't deny themselves anything. Others mess up their marriages or relationships because they can't say no when temptation comes along.

By contrast, Jesus lived a life of denial. He denied the lure of popularity by only ever saying what was right, not what public opinion or the religious authorities wanted to hear. Because of this, one day He might have thousands of people following Him, hanging on His every word because He had fed them all. The next day 99% of them might leave if He said something they didn't like. On one occasion He turned to His disciples and asked, "So are you leaving too?"

Jesus denied Himself excessive comfort. The debate has been raging in the Church for centuries: was Jesus poor or was He rich? Is it a Christian virtue to have nothing, or is it a Christian virtue to prosper? When I examine the Word of God it tells me at every turn that prosperity is offered as a reward for following God and poverty is viewed as a curse. Nowhere do I find a verse that says, "Follow the Lord and you'll have nothing." On the contrary, it is full of promises. The point is, we are to seek God and His kingdom first and foremost, then prosperity and blessing will follow. If we seek after prosperity in and of itself, that is not pleasing to God and we will not find what we are looking for! Jesus could have had anything He wanted, but He made deliberate choices to take only what He needed and to let go of other things.

There were times when Jesus denied Himself certain kinds of companions, such as the rich young ruler who came to Jesus and said, "I'm really impressed with Your teaching.

I love the way You talk about things and I've come to learn." Jesus could have befriended him and spent time with him, but His priority was to invest His life into those who had little and could not repay Him. Worldly non-wisdom would have told Jesus, "Don't offend this guy, he's rich, he could really help fund Your ministry. Think of all the things You could do!" But Jesus was not sucked into this subtle deception. He had a higher goal in mind for the man. Instead he told the guy, "Give it all away, then we can talk." The young man went away sad because he didn't particularly want to part with all his wealth.

Jesus avoided the wrong kind of people, even if they looked like the right kind of people to others. Similarly, we have to be careful how we live and avoid those things that we know won't help us on our journey with God. Incidentally, as far as we know Jesus never said this to another person. I point it out since we could fall into another deception that God hates wealth or people with money. The point was not that the man had money, but that the money had him!

DIRECTION

One word appears several times in James chapter 3. It's the word "peace". James concludes this section by saying, *"And the seed whose fruit is righteousness is sown in peace by those who make peace."*

There are times when I want peace in my house. I've got a mad keen guitarist who lives in my home, two mad keen drummers, and overall, five kids who love music. There are several hi-fi systems that occupy different corners of my home and there are moments when I think, "Just give me some peace!"

But when James is writing about peace he's using a different word. He's not talking about quietness or stillness.

The Greek word that he uses is *eirene* which means the absence of war, harmony, acting at one with others, coming into someone else's success or prosperity and being harmonious.

James is saying that when we live by the wisdom that comes from above we are "harmonious". In other words, "tuned in" to God. By contrast, when we are tuned in to worldly non-wisdom, our lives create a discord. I don't like not being properly tuned into a radio station. I struggle to listen and after a while it begins to grate. Church is like that when we are not tuned into God.

But when you find peace with God you find peace with yourself.

Listen to this little story:

Once upon a time all the animals decided they must do something heroic to meet the challenges of a new world so they organised a school. They adopted an activity curriculum consisting of running, climbing, swimming and flying. To make it easier to administer, all animals took all the subjects.

The duck was excellent at swimming, better in fact than his instructor, and he made excellent grades in flying, but he was very poor at running. Since he was bad at running he had to stay behind after school and drop swimming to practise his running. He kept this up until his webbed feet were badly worn and eventually he was only average at swimming. But average was acceptable at the school, so nobody worried about that fact except the duck.

The rabbit started at the top of the class for running, but had a nervous breakdown because of all the pressure put upon him to start swimming.

The squirrel was excellent at climbing until he developed frustration in the flying class because the teacher made him start from the ground up instead of from the top down. He also developed a nervous twitch from overexertion and got a "C" in climbing and a "D" in running. But that was average.

The eagle was a problem child and had to be disciplined severely. In climbing class he beat all the others to the top of the tree, but insisted on using his own way of getting there.

At the end of the year, an abnormal eel who could swim exceedingly well and could also run, climb and fly, had the highest average and was the valedictorian for the year.

You get the point. We live in a world where everyone is trying to conform to everyone else, but God's wisdom says that He made you to be you and He likes you the way you are. God has a unique blueprint, a destiny and a direction for your life. James tells us that the most important thing is for us is to come to a place of harmony with God and cooperate with His plans for our lives. Tuning into God will get you to the place you need to be, the place that was perfectly designed just for you. The closer we align ourselves with biblical values and principles, the better our judgment will be about the world around us.

Two thousand years ago when Jesus hung on the cross at Calvary it was if God took out a huge tuning fork and struck it on that hill. It sent out a resonant note into the history of all mankind that said, "life, hope, destiny". Those who have ears to hear have listened to that sound and realised that their lives were out of tune with God Himself. They had been tuning into a different sound, a sound of discord, a sound of striving, a sound of bitterness, envy, sin and selfish living. All their lives they'd been tuned to that sound, but now from somewhere into their lives came a new sound. They began to tune into this new sound of faith and their lives were changed forever.

James teaches us that worldly wisdom is demonic and destructive, but the moment we submit to heavenly wisdom and attune our hearts and lives to Jesus, we find peace with God and each other. Then, together we strike a resonant note in the earth that begins shattering the strongholds of darkness, pushing back the darkness that has overshadowed our cities. Together in unity, free from strife, the people of God can make inroads for the kingdom of God and accomplish that which God desires us to accomplish.

**"The early Christians did not say
look at what this world has come to,
but look at what has come to this world."**

(E. Stanley Jones)

CHAPTER 6

OVERCOMING OPPRESSION

"Destiny is not a matter of chance, it is a matter of choice.
It is not something to be waited for,
but something to be achieved."
(William Jennings Bryan)

"If you send a donkey on a trip around the world it still comes back as a donkey." This was a comment made by one dad to his son who was planning a year out travelling. I think his dad was saying that an experience won't change you unless there is a complete change of heart. We have a limited ability to change ourselves, but God goes deep, deeper than any one or anything else. While politicians can change human conditions, only Jesus can change human nature.

We read,

"Come now, you rich, weep and howl for your miseries that are coming upon you! Your riches are corrupted, and your garments are moth-eaten. Your gold and silver are corroded, and their corrosion will be a witness against you and will eat your flesh like fire. You have heaped up treasure in the last days. Indeed the wages of the labourers who mowed your fields, which you kept back by fraud, cry out; and the cries of the reapers have reached the ears of the Lord of Hosts. You have lived on the earth in pleasure and luxury; you have fattened your hearts as in a day of slaughter. You have condemned, you have murdered the just; he does not resist you.

Therefore be patient, brethren, until the coming of the Lord. See how the farmer waits for the precious fruit of the earth, waiting patiently for it until it receives the early and latter rain. You also be patient. Establish your hearts, for the coming of the Lord is at hand.

Do not grumble against one another, brethren, lest you be condemned. Behold, the Judge is standing at the door! My brethren, take the prophets, who spoke in the name of the Lord, as an example of suffering and patience. Indeed we count them blessed who endure. You have heard of the perseverance of Job and seen the end intended by the Lord – that the Lord is very compassionate and merciful.

But above all, my brethren, do not swear, either by heaven or by earth or with any other oath. But let your 'Yes' be 'Yes,' and your 'No,' 'No,' lest you fall into judgment."

(JAMES 5:1–12)

Pastor James sits on both sides of the fence with his church. First he sees those who are trying to hold it all together. Every day is a struggle and every mealtime a challenge. I really can empathise with these people. I was brought up in a single-parent home where my mother often held down three jobs to put food on the table. At the same time we would often hide behind the window whenever there was a knock on the door from some debt collector or rent man, for we had no money to pay them. Loan sharks were around then, charging exorbitant interest rates as they preyed on the poor. In my case, my own father was the oppressor. He had taken off with someone else and did the least possible to accept responsibility for his children. We survived on hand-me-downs, help from other relatives and sheer hard work and ingenuity – until God came into our lives and things began to change. The church, thank God, was, in my own experience, the positive agent for that change. James felt a deep compassion for people like this. Maybe he had child-hood memories of his dad's death and older brother Jesus holding the family together. Maybe he remembered tables and chairs carefully crafted for some inn keeper but never paid for. Either way, his letter contains more than advice, it contains deep heartfelt counsel.

On the other hand James does what the Bible tells him to do, he speaks up for those who can not speak up for themselves. He becomes a voice for the voiceless. He unreservedly denounces the oppressors of the poor, reminding them that Judgment Day is coming. Tough talk when many of them will have been in his church. Hardly the way to win friends and influence people! But how do we use our influence? Who are we speaking up for?

The truth is we cannot sub-contract our responsibility to the poor and remain silent while others in our world suffer. It's great if you can send your pounds and dollars to aid the poor in Africa or India, but you cannot and must not sub-contract your own personal responsibility. Your life must touch theirs, just like Jesus touched yours! You cannot say "It's not my ministry" or even "I make the money". In your making of money you use people! Are they hurting people, lost people, helpless people? Who's skin are you touching?

We change while helping them change. It is the law of life. Oppression is defined as,

- To cause distress
- To lie heavy upon
- To treat with tyrannical cruelty
- To load with heavy burdens

This describes our world, stained by sin and corrupted by Satan and selfish people. People are oppressed by guilt on the inside and then by others on the outside, and God hates it.

I walked around the streets of my city one night asking God for the quickest way to help the most people. He spoke to me about Destiny Angels, a project we now run. In short, it is a helpline number which has, as its strap line, "Nowhere to turn for help? Ask an angel to help you." People phone and we answer. Anyone who calls gets help – no strings attached. Whether callers are straight, gay, young, old, Moslem or Christian, a volunteer army of trained "angel" church folk respond.

I realised that many in my city were like I and my family were years ago. People either not wanting hand-outs, or else fall through the cracks of government support. Maybe they don't have a friend or a relation in the world. May God help us do more.

There are three important principles James chapter 5 teaches us about oppression:

1. We need to step back and evaluate the situation
2. We need to employ the right conduct
3. We should always expect the hand of God to help us.

Applying these three principles will help us overcome oppression.

WE NEED TO EVALUATE

There is not a follower of Christ anywhere in the world who will not, at one time or another, suffer from oppression of some sort themselves. The kind of oppression that James was referring to here was oppression from an employer. He speaks about a scenario in which there were numerous labourers working extremely hard to try to make a living, but they were being paid miserably whilst their employers were getting fat and rich on the fruit of their labours.

In those days, countless people lived on the breadline, teetering on the precipice of absolute poverty. It was normal practice for labourers to be paid on a daily basis. They would work all day and then collect their wages from the boss at night. They were so needy that they couldn't wait until the end of the week to be paid, never mind the end of the month. They needed their meagre wages the same day in order to keep on surviving. Without the money they wouldn't be able to put food on the table and that day their family would go hungry.

The workers that James is referring to in this passage are obviously Christians. They had come to faith in Christ, had found God and the abundant life He offers, and yet they were still living in a situation that was far from good. They worked hard all day trying to be responsible, trying to do the right thing just like you and I, to put food on their table, to take care of their families. But they found that at the end of the day the wealthy people they worked for oppressed them by holding back their pay. They would make feeble excuses like, "Come back and work tomorrow and I'll pay you" or "I'll give it to you another day." Days, even weeks, would go by and they still wouldn't be paid. Sometimes out of sheer desperation they would give up and move on to the next labouring job, anything to get money for food. Wicked employers knew this and would accumulate days and days of free labour this way.

So James' audience were experiencing great hardship because of the unjust oppression of their employers. It's just possible that you might be in a similar situation. You may be working your socks off, doing the best you can to excel in your job and further yourself in the workplace, and yet your employer is not treating you fairly, either by not paying you the going rate or perhaps by refusing to promote you. You're experiencing oppression! Just like these people.

But whether it's work related or not, you may be experiencing hassle or difficulty in other areas of your life and you may be wondering why, when you love the Lord, you are suffering from this oppression? The Bible makes it very clear to us that while God Himself is good, the devil is bad. Jesus described him as a thief who has come to do nothing but steal, kill and destroy. The fact is, because you love Jesus, the devil will do all he can to oppress you, hassle you, and take from you all that God intends for you. If he can rob you then he will. If you find yourself being oppressed today, and would like to be free from oppression, the first thing to do is this: *evaluate*. Evaluate and take stock of the situation; try to look at it objectively, aside from your emotions.

When reading James' teaching closely we see that he takes a systematic approach to every issue he touches, and his starting point is always to carefully consider the situation. James has a three-pronged approach: he evaluates things, he talks about the appropriate biblical response, and then he shows what God will do in the situation. James is showing us an excellent biblical pattern here, because so often we get it mixed up, back to front or the wrong way around! When we are faced with an issue we tend to respond straight away and it is usually an emotional response; we haven't thought things through. If not that, then we will cry out to God to do something – anything – immediately, and fail to learn how to rule and come through in the situation.

James doesn't do that, and I recommend we follow his lead. Whether he is looking at how to overcome troubles, trials, temptation or a negative lifestyle, the first thing he does is draw a line and say, "Let's stop for a moment and look at this. What is happening here, Lord? ... OK, I see, actually, this is what is going on." We have to become disciplined in order to do this. In effect, we are stepping back from the problem momentarily and asking for God's opinion on the matter before we formulate our own response.

This is very important. If you are anything like I am, you will have found yourself at times going through challenges, enduring oppression, sometimes at the hands of other people, and you will have been very tempted to adopt the other person's attitude and begin to act like they are acting. If someone expresses anger at you, it's very easy to be angry back. If someone treats you really unfairly, then it's easy to do the same! But if people act ugly, it does not give us the right to act ugly too!

Have you ever been there? If so, first of all, don't panic – you are not alone! Read Psalm 73 and you'll see that David experienced exactly the same thing. Paraphrasing his words, he says, "I gave up and jacked it all in because I looked at the influence and the wealth of the unrighteous and said to myself, 'What's the point? They are doing all this bad stuff and look what they're getting! Why am I trying to be good and different?' "

I don't know whether these oppressors were sitting in the meeting when James' letter was read out or whether they got hold of it and read it later, but one thing was for sure: the Christians who were being oppressed heard and understood God's viewpoint on the matter. Like them, we need to remember that whatever a man sows, so shall he reap. For that reason alone it is pointless trying to adopt the world's approach. We cannot say, "If I'm greedy and aggressive and tread on other people too, then everything will work out for me . . . " No it won't, because your end will be the same as their end! A lifestyle like that is not pleasing to God.

I recently discovered that aeroplanes have an "attitude". Apparently this describes the relational lines between the wings, the tail and the ground. The planes need to have the right "attitude" when approaching a landing. We find the same thing in life: great landings come from great attitudes! According to Victor Frankel who suffered so much in the death camps of Nazi Germany, his attitude was the one thing that his oppressors could not take away from him. They could do what they liked, but he chose how he responded.

So before we move on with a situation in life we have to make a good judgment, asking what is right, what is wrong, and then take the right stance. No matter how much pressure comes upon us to compromise, react angrily, or weaken our standards, we need to draw a line and say, "This situation is wrong, but I am going to stand for what is right in the right way, and I'll know what is right, not by everybody else's behaviour, but by what God says. He has the last word."

Recently, I had to have a piece of machinery repaired. We have a lawn tractor to cut our grass and it developed a fault, causing the timing belt to break. It cost good money to fix it. In fact, I'd already had to have the same repair job done on it not that long before. Then, when we got it out to use it for the first time after the repair . . . boom! . . . the fault returned before we had cut even a single blade of grass. I called the repairer and he said he would come over and look at it, then take it away for yet another fix. After a short time of inspecting it he called and told me, "Yes, this is the fault and this is what it'll cost you to put it right." I said, "Wait a minute! I've already paid for this same repair twice! Take another look at it – maybe the part you fitted was faulty?" But he was insistent, "No, no, it must have been you . . . "

Not happy about the situation, I dropped into the business and eventually saw the owner who admitted to me that they had disposed of my "broken" part without really inspecting it. They had made an assumption and the assumption was, "It must be his fault not ours, so he'll have to pay for it!"

So often in life we just react to all that's going on instead of evaluating to see which bit of our life may be "broken". Maybe this particular oppression is something to do with me? It's always good to try and understand before pressing to be understood, and to take note that God has given us two ears and one mouth, so we need to do twice as much listening as talking!

Is it wrong to be rich?

Before we move on to the second stage in James' three-pronged approach, let's make one final observation. One might easily assume from James' scathing attack on the oppressors in this passage that he has it in for the rich. After all, it's not the first time in his epistle that he's had a go at them. One could conclude from his vocabulary that here is biblical evidence that it is wrong to be rich: *"Come now, you rich, weep and howl for your miseries that are coming upon you!"* (James 5:1).

Does James have a problem with people who have wealth? No. There are several people in the New Testament who had great wealth and there are even more people in the Old Testament, but they served God and accomplished His purposes in their generation. This is the heart of James' issue: *"You have lived on the earth in pleasure and luxury; you have fattened your hearts as in a day of slaughter"* (James 5:5). The problem James had with these wealthy individuals wasn't the fact that they had great resources, it was the way they used (or misused) them. He said, "You've got *so much*, but look how you've spent it on everything you could possibly want and more besides." The principle that James is pointing to is this: the more you have, the more is required from you. Looking at it another way: the more God entrusts us with, the more we can do with it.

Maybe you are reaching out to God in your business or your job, wanting to prosper, succeed and go forward. If so, make sure that as you strive for prosperity, you realise that the weight of responsibility is on you to use your resources wisely, and that weight will increase according to your increase. Be able to say with a clear conscience, "God, if You bless me I will do even more for You, because I know what's required of me."

The rich, in the days of James, did some ridiculous things with their wealth. I read recently some well-documented historical reports from that time period. One story told of a wealthy Roman businessman who was approached by a theatre company asking if they could borrow some of his clothes in order to put on a show. "Yes," he replied, "I have over 6,000 changes of clothes. Come and help yourselves to whatever you want!" Another story told of how the rich, bored with drinking wine, began to melt down and dilute gold and pearls and drank that instead!

I also read in the newspaper recently of a Saudi Arabian prince who had seventeen wives and who ordered each of them one of the latest Bentleys, each one specially extended and stretched (because they weren't quite long enough) and kitted out with all kinds of non-standard features. The average cost of each car was almost £1,000,000 and the delivery charge alone was £190,000. That's a postage bill and a half!

A couple of weeks ago the accounts were published in the newspaper of one of the members of the Royal Family. This person had given £48,000 to charitable causes in the last year. That sounds great until you see that it represented not even a half of 1% of their annual income! No doubt they thought they were being generous. I think we have kids in our church who are more generous because they give 5p of their 50p pocket money.

All of these are examples of the fact that a small percentage of fabulously wealthy people enjoy an absurd amount of wealth, while a huge percentage of the global population live in abject poverty. But here is what James says: God is not against wealth, He wants us to succeed and prosper. But the more we have, the more is required of us. As our prosperity increases, so should our giving and service. Let's evaluate our situations and see them through God's eyes, measure them by His standards. Even when we are being oppressed, God is still in control. He sees, watches and will respond.

WE NEED TO EMPLOY THE RIGHT CONDUCT

In my attic at home I have a three-legged stool that used to belong to my grandmother. It's a milking stool and she used to use it when she was a kid. On the old flagstone floors and uneven earth of the cowsheds, when it was time to hand-milk the cows, the most stable thing that you could sit on was a three-legged stool. James' solution to oppression is like a solid, three-legged stool. We've looked at one leg of it – here is the second. After evaluating the situation and looking at it from God's perspective, we need to employ the right conduct.

How do we make sure that we conduct ourselves according to God's standards in a given situation – especially when we are being oppressed and not treated well?

The first thing to realise is that we must never underestimate the value that the experience has on our own character. Who you are and what you have become in your life matters most when you are under pressure. If you are being pressurised and oppressed, the strength of your character will be responsible for either keeping you there or causing you to bail out. Twice in these few verses James tells us to lean on our godly character to be patient. We may not like this, but in fact we can turn oppression into a positive growth experience because it builds character.

"Therefore be patient, brethren, until the coming of the Lord . . . You also be patient. Establish your hearts, for the coming of the Lord . . . "

(JAMES 5:7–8)

An interesting thing I noticed when studying this passage is that although in our English translations we use the same word "patience" twice, in the original Greek James uses two different words with subtly different meanings. First of all James uses a phrase which can be translated "stand up strong". In other words, being patient in the face of oppression means to "stand up strong underneath it". Oppression is an outside force that is exerted upon us and which tries to reduce us and make us feel small. The oppression may be circumstantial, emotional, mental or spiritual – but when it comes the temptation for us is to buckle underneath it. James says, "No, stand up under it. Don't lie down!"

So firstly we need to invest in building our character so that when oppression comes we remain determined and strong. We need to be able to say, "No matter what, here I stand. I will not cave in because I know that God is on my side." Instead of saying, "What's the point? I'm jacking it in," we say, "I don't like this, but I'm going to keep going. I'll keep hanging on."

The second phrase James uses can be translated literally as "refuse to run away". So when oppression comes we don't cave in and we don't run away either. When everything inside us is telling us to run, we stand strong and we hold our ground.

Have you ever been in a situation where you've run?

One Sunday morning a man asked for prayer. He told me that he was in sales and he wasn't making any! That's a problem. He said that if he didn't get a breakthrough soon he would lose his job. He had a wife and five kids to feed. I really felt for him. So much so that I said, "Tell you what, not only are we going to pray, but I will fast and pray until you get that breakthrough." He was shocked that someone would care enough to do this. So I did. I didn't eat until Wednesday, taking extra time in prayer for this man and his family to get a breakthrough. Wednesday night I called him.

"So, how's it gone?" I asked.

"How's what gone?" he replied.

"The sales of course!"

At which point he told me that on Monday morning he went in and resigned, thinking it better to jump before he was pushed! Other than wanting to kill him for not telling me, it was obvious that he had just run from the situation! Who knows, maybe he bailed out just as his breakthrough was about to come. Regrettably, he was in the habit of running every time the pressure built.

Sometimes issues in life just make us want to run and there are different kinds of running. Sometimes we run physically – we walk away from situations. Perhaps we decide to quit our job because we don't want to face a particular person or situation. Or we take time off sick when we're not really sick. Some of us run mentally – we can't physically go anywhere so we try to escape in our mind. We fantasise that things are different in order to numb ourselves from reality, because we don't want to face it.

The way we react to oppression is so important. We mustn't crumble and we mustn't run away from it. Neither can we blame anyone else for it. James warns us against this:

"Do not grumble against one another, brethren, lest you be condemned. Behold, the Judge is standing at the door!"

(JAMES 5:9)

A common reaction when we are feeling pressurised and oppressed is to take it out on other people. When we are being squeezed, squashed and we're feeling very uncomfortable, we can't do anything to stop the oppression, so what do we do? Find an easy target and hit it! Sad to say, when we are under great pressure, it's usually our family and friends who find themselves on the wrong end of a bad attitude. You can be doing something normal with your family, someone says something innocently and the next minute you explode with a mighty overreaction to the situation.

What has happened? You've just increased the territory of the thing that is oppressing you! So instead of being oppressed in one area of your life, now you have given it access to your marriage or your relationship with your kids or your friends etc. When we hit out at others because we're feeling oppressed we give the oppression the power to affect us in other areas that are nothing to do with it.

If we employ the right conduct we soon discover that where our attitudes go, our mouths will follow. James concludes his advice to the believers by saying,

"Do not swear, either by heaven or by earth or with any other oath. But let your 'Yes' be 'Yes,' and your 'No,' 'No,' lest you fall into judgment."

(JAMES 5:12)

He is saying that when we are under oppression and pressure we shouldn't be hasty or impulsive. That way we won't find ourselves on the wrong side of God – the very person who is trying to help us – or making rash promises to others.

> **"The framework has been created
> in which the greatest thing in the world
> can emerge by choice – character."**
>
> (E. Stanley Jones)

EXPECT THE HAND OF GOD

There's a little proverb in the book of Ecclesiastes that says, *"a threefold cord is not quickly broken"* (Ecclesiastes 4:12). We often use that picture in relation to marriage: with a husband, wife and God you've got a winning team. Similarly, James' strategy for overcoming oppression has three strands to it, and this is the third: don't forget God!

Everything takes on a different dimension when God gets involved. This what we read in James 5:11. I just love this verse:

> *"Indeed we count them blessed who endure. You have heard of the perseverance of Job and seen the end **intended by the Lord**."*
>
> (emphasis added)

Whatever the nature of the oppression that you are experiencing, know this: God has an end for the situation. God has planned a blessed outcome for you, however bleak things may appear at the moment. God has an "end" in mind for every area of your life: your business, your relationships, your marriage, your ministry. James uses Job as an example because he went through so many trials and difficulties, yet in the end it all worked out fine. Job ended up with twice as much and a whole book in the Bible written for our benefit. Sometimes when we're in the midst of oppression and pressure we lose sight of the fact that God has a plan; He has an end in mind.

Victory – that's what God has in mind.

> *"But thanks be to God, who always leads us in triumph in Christ, and manifests through us the sweet aroma of the knowledge of Him in every place."*
>
> (2 CORINTHIANS 2:14 NASB)

God is executing a plan for your life that is destined to be successful. He has in mind your prosperity and wellbeing. He has not made any strategic plans for your failure! We need to remember that God never calls us to go through something in which He cannot keep us, and never asks us to do something for which He does not equip us. In the place of oppression it may appear to us that God is somewhere distant, but He's not. He is there with us, working everything out. Maybe you're being oppressed right now and you've asked God to get you out of there. He will at the right time. Delay is not denial.

Three times in these verses James refers to God as the Judge – the first ever title given to God in the Bible. He encourages the oppressed to keep their hope alive because Jesus is returning soon – this time not as a suffering servant, but as the King of Glory. The early Church always referred to themselves as being in "the last days". Well, if they were in the last days, we are in the last of the last days. But I think James is also talking about a different kind of coming. He's not just talking about the Second Coming, he's talking about Jesus coming into the midst of our oppression and being there with us, assuring us that, although things are unfair now, He will pass judgment in due course and everything will be set right.

James, as Jesus' brother, would have seen or heard of Him operating in so many situations: raising people from the dead, praying for the supernatural multiplication of food, performing various other creative miracles, healing

countless people. In each of these situations what he saw
was, "The Lord coming". James' message to his people and
to us is: stand strong, don't run away from it, stay godly,
and expect God to come. And God will surely come into the
midst of your situation. His aim is that through these
circumstances you will be transformed from the inside out
and made more and more into the likeness of His Son.

> **"Change is the law of life and
> those who only look to the past or present
> are certain to miss the future."**
> (John F. Kennedy)

OVERCOMING SICKNESS AND WEAKNESS

"The whole of life depends
as much on desire for life here
as the truth of a settled personality."
(J. Mahaputra)

Imagine that I am driving down the road in a two-tonne truck. Unwittingly I exceed the speed limit, use my mobile phone while driving and jump a red light. A nearby police officer standing on an intersection notices this. He calmly steps out into the road stands in front of my approaching

124

CHAPTER 7

OVERCOMING SICKNESS AND WEAKNESS

*"The wealth of past experience
is made available for the future
as the wealth of untried possibilities."*
(J. Moltmann)

Imagine that I am driving down the road in a two-tonne truck. Unwittingly, I exceed the speed limit, use my mobile phone while driving and jump a red light. A nearby police officer standing on an intersection notices this. He calmly steps out into the road stands in front of my approaching truck and puts his hand up, indicating I should stop. He is apprehensive and the adrenaline is flowing through his body for this just happens to be his first day on foot patrol. In fact, he is a new recruit, just out of college. He remembers that he should show confidence and take control of the situation. And so this thin, young man tries to stop my two-tonne vehicle. Who do you think has the greatest power? Me and my truck or the policeman?

The truth is, I do!

My truck is immeasurably more powerful than an 11 stone police officer. But the important question is not who has the most power, but who has the most authority?

Although I could run him over, he has the Queen's crown on his hat and lapels and as such he operates under her authority. The Queen and her Government who appointed him are fully prepared to back him up. If necessary with all the might of the armed forces. Knowing this, his authority causes me to rein in my power and stop.

The verses of James 5:13–18 focus particularly on sickness and reveal some powerful truths. The word James uses for "sickness" is the Greek word *astheneo* (from which we derive the word "asthma"). It means more than just being sick. It speaks of being weak, feeble, infirm, impotent or living well below our normal vitality levels.

So the teaching here does not just apply to those who are physically sick. It includes those who may be emotionally sick or just feeling weak and struggling to get through life; who perhaps seem to go from one difficulty to the next or constantly have ailments of one kind or another.

So often we think that these real-life issues create a contest, and that the contest is power verses power. Me against the devil or the sicknesses and challenges I face. But it's not that at all. It's power verses authority, and he who has the most authority wins every time, especially when he also has the power to back it up.

Jesus said,

> *"And He said to them, 'I was watching Satan fall from heaven like lightning. Behold I have given you **authority** to tread on serpents and scorpions, and over all the **power** of the enemy, and nothing shall injure you.'"*
>
> (LUKE 10:18–19 NASB, emphasis added)

Jesus gives His authority to those who follow Him. Even the newest recruit has the same potential as a serious heavy-weight prophet like Elijah. Like the policeman we can put up our hand and say, "Stop!" Further, not only can we operate in this authority, but James calls in reinforcements when it comes to sickness. He says, "Get the elders! Those who should know who they are, whose they are, and how this works."

James writes,

> *"Is anyone among you suffering? Let him pray. Is anyone cheerful? Let him sing psalms. Is anyone among you sick? Let him call for the elders of the church, and let them pray over him, anointing him with oil in the name of the Lord. And the prayer of faith will save the sick, and the Lord will raise him up. And if he has committed sins, he will be forgiven. Confess your trespasses to one another, and pray for one another, that you may be healed. The effective, fervent prayer of a righteous man avails much. Elijah was a man with a nature like ours, and he prayed earnestly that it would not rain; and it did not rain on the land for three years and six months. And he prayed again, and the heaven gave rain, and the earth produced its fruit."*
>
> (JAMES 5:13–18)

So how do we use this authority?

ASK!

In these few verses the word "prayer" occurs seven times, so it is obvious that prayer is very important to James in the point he is trying to make. Here we find all kinds of praying people: praying Christians, praying elders, praying friends and a praying prophet. Prayer is the greatest use of authority.

Imagine I met you one day and said, "Let's have a coffee." You would perhaps think, that's nice, but hey, we're all so busy. But if I said to you twice or three times when I met you, "Come on, let's have a coffee," you would think, "This guy is serious." What if I said it to you five times in one conversation, what would you think then? You would think, "He really, really means it!"

Well Jesus, in one conversation, says five times, *"Whatever you ask the Father in My name I will do it"* (see John chapter 14).

Do you think He meant it?

CENTRE

We all have a centre, a focal point around which our lives revolve. Many things shout for our attention, looking to be the centre point of our lives. They include our thoughts, our words and our actions. The centre becomes the centre-piece of most of our conversations.

> **"You can locate people by what they say; their confession locates them."**
>
> (K. Hagin)

It seems to me that many people in my home country of Wales are consumed by death. They always want to tell me who's died. Once my aunt told me of old Mr Thomas who had suddenly died. When I asked what he died of she replied "Oh, nothing serious!"

James asks the question, *"Is anyone among you suffering?* [undergoing hardship] *Let him pray. Is anyone cheerful? Let him sing psalms."* The first thing that James wants to underline is this: no matter what direction our life is taking, our focus should always be God-ward. Have you got a problem? Then call on Him. Are there good things happening in your life? Then thank Him, because He is the source of your life. This is simple but profound advice.

The centre of our lives must not be our problems – no matter how loud they shout. The centre of our lives must be God. And we must, wilfully, deliberately, consciously keep Him there!

For a long time people thought that the sun revolved around the earth, until a man called Copernicus came along and proved otherwise. The earth actually revolves around the sun. The world is not about us – it's about *Him*, and when we get the centre right everything else is right!

People who call on God only when they have problems or when a crisis occurs are worshipping Jesus of the Genie lamp. We only rub it when we need Him! Very often, when things are going well and we are blessed, we forget to keep connected to God. James says, yes, call on God in a crisis – that's the right thing to do – but don't forget to give thanks when you are being blessed. It's a good discipline to develop, when something goes right in our life, to say, "Thank You, Father."

Maybe James had been through enough seasons with his church members at crisis time – cried with them, prayed with them, taught them and helped them – only to see that when the going gets good, the good get going – right out of church life and into the distant blue yonder! Rather, God wants us to live under an open heaven called grace, and learning to thank, love and honour Him in the good times keeps us there. If we see that God is good and not just the answer to my life, but the very source of it, that keeps us in a great place.

> **"The man who comes to a right belief of God is relieved of ten thousand temporal problems."**
> (A.W. Tozer)

ENERGISED

We read,

> *"The effective, fervent prayer of a righteous man avails much."*
> (JAMES 5:16)

Another translation renders it this way, *"The prayer of a righteous man is powerful when **energised**"* and could be rephrased like this: "The energised prayer of a righteous man is powerful and effective."

To energise something means, "to give energy to it; to activate or invigorate; to raise to a higher energy level." In physics it can also refer to the process of exciting atoms – which literally means getting them bouncing off one another so that their energy levels are caught, transmitted and consequently increased.

Have you noticed how some people can appear very quiet and subdued, but get them onto their pet subject and suddenly they become animated? My son is a prime example. Talk about homework or the need to study for forthcoming exams and I get, "Ummm ... aaah ... yes, Dad." But if I start talking about some of his favourite music – Steve Vai or Joe Satriani – then **boom**, we're into another orbit and suddenly he is energised. Something has taken him to another level. People are like these atoms. They too can be "excited".

Look at it this way: today CD drives, DVD players and other optical devices using laser technology have become very common. Laser technology is big business. Lasers work by utilising energy and passing it on. The word "laser" is an acronym which stands for Light Amplification by Stimulated Emission of Radiation. Imagine that a beam of pure light could melt something as hard as steel! The following quote explains how stimulating atoms creates a laser beam:

"Atoms and molecules exist at low and high energy levels. Those at low levels can be excited to higher levels, usually by heat, and after reaching the higher levels they give off light as they return to the lower level. In ordinary light sources the many excited atoms or molecules emit light independently and in many different colours or wavelengths.

If, however, during the brief instant that an atom is excited light of a certain wavelength impinges on it and the atom can be stimulated to emit radiation that is in phase or in step with the wave that's stimulated it.

The new emission thus augments or amplifies the passing wave and makes it more powerful than ever before. And if the phenomenon can be multiplied sufficiently the resulting beam is made up of wholly coherent or single frequency light that the effect will be tremendous and powerful."

So, imagine a little atom. He's not very excited and having a "low energy" day. But along comes another atom who is a lot more powerful and energetic. This gets the first atom very excited and he begins to shake. He shakes and shakes until he is vibrating at the same frequency as the other atom. Maybe he goes on and does the same to another, until they are all it. When this happens we get laser beams. When people do it we get "church" and stuff happens there! The laser beam of faith cuts through the hard steel of sickness and weakness.

Why am I telling you all this? Because we can all hit low points, sometimes desperately low. When you feel low, weak, feeble, sick and lacking the vital-life kind of energy, you need an "energy" of a higher order to come and revitalise you. James says that although the fact may be that you are sick, there is a *higher order of truth* that supersedes it – the truth of God's Word which results in power. All lasers need an originating source of power. God's Word is that power! Note the Bible points out faith comes by *hearing* not reading! When we hear the word it starts up that oscillating process. It gets the energy of faith moving. God can and does heal sick bodies, sick minds, sick lives and even sick nations! And the key to seeing God do this is effective prayer – prayer that is energised by the Word and raises the temperature spiritually so that the vibrancy of life is increased. This kind of prayer, James says, is powerful and effective.

A low energy atom always possesses the potential to be a high energy atom, even if it isn't one to begin with. The possibility is always there. When the energy of God's Word kicks in it produces power, and this power is more than enough to deal with any sickness or infirmity known to man. Today, so many people formulate their theology according to their experience, but this is a wrong approach. We should base our beliefs on what the Bible actually says – and this *is* what it says! Power can be released to us in prayer and it will strengthen, heal and equip us – so we'd better believe it.

Atoms, once excited, eventually lose energy and need to be recharged to operate at that higher level once more. To me, this is a picture of one of the key reasons the Church exists. Church is one of the places we go to be recharged.

The preaching of God's Word and praise and worship are all designed to energise us by re-centring our lives around the source of all power. No matter how much energy we have expended in living life and serving God, we can be renewed, refreshed and re-energised as we gather together with God's people. Moody said, "I leak, so I need to be filled daily."

POSITIONED FOR POWER

You cannot become a Christian without believing in the supernatural. Jesus was born via a virgin birth. Even with all the advancements in science they still can't do that! It's impossible, it's miraculous, it's supernatural. Yet, if Jesus was not born of a virgin, then He would be a sinner like me, and even if He was still willing to die for my sins, it would not be enough. He, like Muhammad, Buddha and all others, would have had to die for His own sins.

Secondly, we have the little incident we call the resurrection. Jesus was physically raised from the dead and lives today. If you don't believe or can't accept these foundational premises, you are, for sure, not a Christian. The weight of Scripture is against you. Besides, who is there who can save you? A sinful, dead Jesus can't! But if these things are the starting blocks to your faith, then we must continue as we have begun – believing in the miraculous. It's absurd and completely illogical to say that you have confidence that your sins are forgiven, that you pray to a living Jesus and that you are confident about a place in Heaven, and then at the same time try to argue (without any weight from Scripture) that healings and the like are no more! God backs up His authority with power.

So what about this power? How does this power work to produce healing? How does it work to overcome weakness? How does it work to produce change?

First, we need to understand that the source of the power is beyond us, but it can operate in imperfect people – like us! James uses a wonderful phrase when he refers to Elijah, saying that, *"He was a man like us."* One translation says, *"He was a man of similar passions."* What James wants us to know is that Elijah, regarded by many as being at the pinnacle of effective prayer, was just an ordinary guy. He was no different from you and me.

When we read the story of Elijah we discover he saw mighty miracles and the power of God breaking through, but we also discover that he suffered from depression, was prone to fear, and got tired and confused at times. In other words, he felt all the things that you and I feel. But just look at his life: fire from heaven and rain for the earth! We need to get connected to the same heavenly grid.

The apostle Paul considered one situation worse than any other: to live *"having no hope and without God in the world"* (Ephesians 2:12).

It is possible to know God and still live as if you didn't! Simply by leaving Him out. But why live without God when you can live with Him?

And when you live with Him, so often the worst and the weakest can become the mightiest. Spurgeon said of Mary Magdalene, "Grace found her a maniac and made her a minister!"

Smith Wigglesworth, who was used by God to perform so many healings and mighty miracles said, "I'm one hundred times bigger on the inside than I am on the outside." Wigglesworth understood that due to his position in Christ he had an inner power and it was that power which changed things.

Who you are matters more than what you do! The Bible contains many "mirror verses" – things we should look at regularly to see who we are!

Here is one passage of "mirror verses":

"Therefore, if anyone is in Christ, he is a new creation; old things have passed away; behold, all things have become new. Now all things are of God, who has reconciled us to Himself through Jesus Christ, and has given us the ministry of reconciliation, that is, that God was in Christ reconciling the world to Himself, not imputing their trespasses to them, and has committed to us the word of reconciliation.

Now then, we are ambassadors for Christ, as though God were pleading through us: we implore you on Christ's behalf, be reconciled to God. For He made Him who knew no sin to be sin for us, that we might become the righteousness of God in Him."

(2 CORINTHIANS 5:17–21)

Years ago, Goldie Hawn starred in a film called *Overboard*. She is an heiress, enjoying a party on her private yacht, when she becomes drunk and falls overboard. She ends up washed up onto a beach. Then, along comes a man who happens to be a single dad, and a bit of a loafer, who finds and rescues her – kind of! Because she hit her head as she fell overboard she has temporary amnesia. The guy leads her to believe that she is his wife and that her duties are to clean his house, raise his kids, do all his cooking and generally slave for him – all of which she does for several months following, not realising who she is!

Eventually, however, her memory returns and she discovers and then remembers who she is – a very rich lady who has cooks, cleaners and other servants working for *her*. When she finds out the truth she cries, "Aaaarrrghhh! What have I been doing?!"

It has a very happy ending. They fall in love and they both change to the benefit and joy of the kids. She loses her "life is all about me" outlook and he loses his "life is to be simply survived" mentality.

Michael Griffiths in his book *Cinderella with Amnesia*[1] argues that the Church is like this heiress with amnesia. The Church has had something akin to a knock on the head and we've forgotten who we are. Paul's statement in Corinthians helps put things back into perspective. As Christians, children of God, our size, relative weakness, or cleverness, is irrelevant. It's the size of our God that counts!

Making the Right Connection

You may not feel like a powerful Christian today (I don't think Elijah did most of the time), but it's not about what you feel! The fact that you don't *feel* like you have spiritual power and authority doesn't change anything, because your position in Christ remains secure. God's power works in your life because of your position, but it will only continue to work if you stay connected.

The power of God is much like electricity in that regard. I have an electrical supply coming into my home because I have the right connections. But before the electricity company would pump power into my home, I had to open an account with them and become a registered user. Once they had all my details they were willing to supply me with the power.

James writes about making and, most importantly, keeping the right connections in order to keep the power flowing in our lives.

How to Stay Connected

1. Remember that you are a needy person!

James stresses the importance of confessing our sins to one another. Confessing in a box to a priest in secret is one thing, but confessing our sins to each other is a whole different ball game. The first example is not biblical, the second is! But is it really safe to get this close to people? Those in ministry are especially vulnerable. Having been stabbed in the back, probably many times, ministers can soon learn: if you want a friend, buy a dog! Ministers can end up on pedestals, beyond reach and beyond approach, but not beyond temptation. We are all needy, we need each other's care and concern. All of those famous weapons in the Ephesians 6 arsenal are for forward advance, there is nothing for my back. That is where my brother comes in! I need him to watch out for my blind spots. We cannot expose ourselves to everyone in our lives to the same degree, that would be foolish, but we must let some in! Church history is littered with people who learned how to move in power with God to see healings and miracles – but failed to see the power of God at work in their marriage or in the lives of their kids. In those areas, God was left out, and they soon became the Achilles heel which eventually took them out. Don't let that happen to you.

Could you call for an elder to pray for you if you needed to? TV shows may have prayer partners, but only the Church has elders. Turning on is not enough – you must turn out. Elders are officers commissioned by God to help you. James says call for them. Don't wait for the home visit – go and get them! How serious are you about getting well? Elders have already been told by God that they should be teaching the Word – that faith-producing, oscillating Word. Then, over and above the laying on of hands, we are told they should anoint with oil. This makes the moment a special occasion. Oil anointing is a throw-back to ancient times. Every time it happened God showed up. Oil anointing was reserved for special people on special occasions, kings and priests usually, setting them apart for office and enduing them with power. Well, it seems as if God thinks you and I are special enough to enjoy its privileges, and there is no moment more special than when you get healed! Being able to call for elders is a good sign that you are not only growing in authority – you are under it too. God sees His leaders as an umbrella for His people. He put them there as protection for us.

So many find it hard to submit to any man's authority, until they need that man, maybe to pray the prayer of healing over them. It's easier to submit to a God we can't see than an imperfect man we can see.

Others confuse submission with agreement. My kids submit to me when I say, "Let's go to the cinema and buy lots of sweets."

"You're the man, dad! We submit to you!"

But when I say, "OK, it's time for bed ... homework ... " etc., it's another story. Staying connected means staying safe. Staying safe means being accountable, not just agreeable.

2. Honour what God honours

There is only one thing Jesus is coming back for and that's the Church. He loves it, died for it and will come for it. Touch the Church and you touch God. One particular warning in the New Testament carries the label: "Danger, can seriously harm your health". Paul in 1 Corinthians speaks of not appreciating or discerning the Lord's body when we break bread. He also encourages us to judge ourselves. To put it bluntly, he says if you have a problem with another Christian, sort it out! Whether it's your fault or theirs, take care of it. Jesus taught the same thing in Matthew 5 and Matthew 18. Whoever started it, we each have the responsibility to do all we can to stop it and bring a peaceful conclusion. Abusing the church body can lead to problems with our body. Bad attitudes create bad health. *"Envy rots the bones"* says Proverbs 14:30 (NIV).

3. See the bigger picture

Some things are connected even if we think they shouldn't be. According to Peter, problems with your wife will lead to problems with your prayer life (1 Peter 3:7). We may not think that fair, but God thinks it's right. The only promise of a long and healthy life comes with a condition attached: honour your father and your mother (Ephesians 6:2–3). Why in the world should these things be so intertwined by God, it's just not fair! Parents, marriage and church are all relationships considered by God to be important. They are an expression of His Father heart. He wants a family and wants the family together. The Bible calls it unity. Some want to get it together with the church down the road when they can't get it together with the guy across the pew from them.

My car has a rev counter with an area marked in red. Drive the car in that zone and you will have problems. Similarly, we are not built to take our bodies into the red zone of poor, irresponsible relationships. Overcoming weaknesses and sickness is inextricably linked to the way in which we connect with others.

APPLYING THE POWER
TO OVERCOME SICKNESS

Here are some practical guidelines that will help you as you seek to see God's power at work in your life.

1. Never talk about your problem, but talk to it.

Our words have tremendous power and we need to be careful how we use them. Our words can cause our faith level to rise, but they can also sap us of faith when we use negative words. Remember what we said about "the wheel of our Genesis?" Our words create worlds, and they will create your world.

In Mark 11:23 Jesus said,

"Whoever says to this mountain, 'Be removed and be cast into the sea,' and does not doubt in his heart, but believes that those things he says will be done, he will have whatever he says."

Most of us have been conditioned to talk *about* our problems, but instead of talking about them let's talk *to* them.

2. If you are in a situation, never claim it to be yours
We too readily accept affliction when it comes upon us. We talk in terms of *my* sickness, *my* cold, *my* headache etc. Don't claim these things as yours. They don't belong to you, they are alien invasions into your body. Instead, keep praying and refuse to think about accepting the sickness. They are always an "it". It's not a part of me.

3. Pray the Word not the problem
In Isaiah 43:26 we read this: God says,

> *"Put Me in remembrance;*
> *Let us contend together;*
> *State your case, that you may be acquitted."*

So often, when we come to pray, we pour out our distress and troubles before God. We pour out our feelings and emotions, because that's where we're at. But remember one of the first things that we learnt when we began to study the book of James: God does not, first of all, respond to your tears, or to your pain, or to your distress; God responds to *faith*.

Instead you can pray, "Lord, You said that You are the Lord who heals us! You said that You'd never leave me or forsake me! You said..." without it being arrogant and presumptuous. This is what the words in Isaiah mean – you can state your case before God. When you remind God of His own words it demonstrates that you actually believe what He has said. When you begin to pray like that your life will take on a new dimension. The devil is brilliant at building glass ceilings – putting limits on our prayers – but we need to remove the limits from our minds and realise that God can do anything He wants, and He actually wants to answer our prayers!

More than 35,000 people have attended healing meetings with us in Scotland over the last five years. The BBC, ITV, *Daily Mail,* and many other newspapers and magazines have reported on these things. God heals sick people.

My God is not only able, He is willing.

When God wanted to make Himself known to us He had a problem. What language could He use, how could He describe Himself? It's like me telling an ant what I am like – only more so! God uses names. He has the longest list of names of anyone I know. But the names not only tell us what to call Him, but tell us what He is in *essence* and *nature.* He once said He is *"Jehovah-Repheka"*: I am the Lord who healeth thee (Exodus 15:26). He went further and personified Himself amongst us. God became man. Jesus was hugely preoccupied with healing people. He has not changed. So why settle for less when God wants you to have more?

> **"God is as large as you allow Him to be.**
> **He is also as small as you confine Him to be."**
>
> (David Yonggi Cho)

Notes

1. Michael Griffiths, *Cinderella with Amnesia: Practical Discussions of the Relevance of the Church,* Inter-Varsity Press, 1975.

CHAPTER 8

OVERCOMING FOR OTHERS

"You and I ought not to die
before we have explained ourselves to one another."
(John Adams, speaking to Thomas Jefferson)

I see it all the time. People come in late and leave just before the end of the church meeting. They want to be there, but they don't want to connect – not just yet, anyway. Noticing this, I and my associate pastors, on occasions, have reinstated an age-old church tradition and begun standing at the door before the end of each meeting to say our thank you's and goodbyes.

That's not easy when there are many people and multiple meetings. But on so many occasions people's stories have begun to emerge. A story of divorce here, abuse there; an illicit affair or a partner hooked on some chemical dependency. Some who are on a spiritual journey, but who have not arrived at their destination yet. Occasionally there are ordinary folks, just checking us out. Others carry some hurt turned to sadness or bitterness and are looking for answers or healing. But they come. Then the miracle begins to happen. They come on time, even a few minutes early, and stay around at the end. Somehow, in some way, God has been at work, healing, changing, restoring and forgiving. And eventually they begin to turn into the champions mentioned in an earlier chapter, like Olympians wearing the *stephanos* – the laurel crown. Instead of being down and out they are up and in!

Paul spoke of them in Romans, "conquerors" he called them. But wait, Paul said something more: *"More than conquerors"* he called them. So how does the "more than" bit work? It happens when not only have we come through with God's help, but now we are helping others through. "More than" conquerors turn their pain into someone else's healing. They share their mistakes to help someone else learn a quicker lesson. They sit at tables, meet in coffee houses doing life together – not just chatting about the news, sport or shopping, but going deeper, going where it feels so vulnerable, but where change happens.

Having taught us how to do life, James puts the finishing touches on his message and says,

"Dear brothers, if anyone has slipped away from God and no longer trusts the Lord, and someone helps him understand the Truth again, that person who brings him back to God will have saved a wandering soul from death, bringing about the forgiveness of many sins."

(JAMES 5:19–20 LB)

The help that others need may not only be found in the counselling room, but in the living room and the locker room, where people, ordinary people, start doing what Adams and Jefferson wanted to do: "explain themselves" to one another. Only this is not about politics, it is about life; it is the challenges and solutions found in this leader of all leaders, Jesus. It's a higher order of life than just gossip and chat – it's a lifeline from Heaven carried best by those who have received from this grace the most.

The great reformer, Martin Luther, did not like James' letter, calling it "an epistle of straw". He even doubted at times whether it should have been included in the Bible at all. Luther lived and worked against a backdrop of Catholic indulgences, sold for a penny for the forgiveness of weary souls. He fought those who went on pilgrimages and filled their days with penances in search of peace. He hated with a vengeance the clergy who manipulated the needs and the ignorance of the people to satisfy their own sordid ends. Nothing, he thought, should be added to the Gospel he had come to see and love. In it he found total acceptance and righteousness through faith and by grace in Christ.

But it appears he misunderstood where James was coming from. James was not adding to the Gospel, but unpacking it, leaving a trail of "how to's" and correct responses to wrong situations. He also held up the gold standard of authentic Christianity, a "royal law" he called it. If this thing is real then it really works. The proof of the pudding is in the eating and the taste of this cake is love in all its fullness. Not a wishy washy, flaky, emotional, come-and-go kind of love, but a love that loves the unlovable, that goes where it doesn't want to go, and is bothered enough to make a difference. You only overcome when you help others overcome too!

*"Yes indeed, it is good when you truly obey our Lord's command,
'You must love and help your neighbours just as much as you love
and take care of yourself.'"*

(JAMES 2:8 LB)

So, in concluding here are five top tips in the overcomer's
master class.

LIVE BEYOND YOUR MEANS

The names of God are used 1,900 times in the Bible, and
there are over 20,000 references to Him. The Bible contains
more than 3,000 promises including, *"I will never leave you nor
forsake you"* and *"greater is he that is in you than he who is against
you."* Jesus, at all times, was trying to get His disciples to have
a "multitude mindset" and to develop "you have got more
than you need" thinking.

He must have laughed when He, a carpenter, told the
fishermen how to catch fish: "Put the nets down on
the other side." They caught so many it nearly sank two
boats. On another occasion Jesus told these same men,
"You feed them," as they looked out at 10,000+ people.
"With what?" they wanted to know, but then spent all
evening picking up the leftovers from the banquet. Before
all this took place Jesus had ordered some servants to, "Fill
the pots with water," and when the contents were poured
out the pots contained vintage wine. Later, telling the
parable of the prodigal son, Jesus puts the words into
the delinquent son's mouth, saying, "There is more than
enough in My Father's house."

In his letter James covers all of life's eventualities and
shows us a vivid picture of this "more than" God, the One
who is all-sufficient. Whatever challenges arise we have got
whatever it takes to tackle them because He supplies our
needs. This includes grace, patience, wisdom strength and

confidence. The key then, is not to live within our limits, but to live within His. Communion with God is not a chore or a duty, but a lifeline. I once watched with fascination as a lifeboat unloaded supplies to an island lighthouse in severe, rough seas. They pulled the goods to and fro on the connecting ropes. God wants to put His life in you and send it through you, not just "park you up" for the exit call.

There is no way we would ever know anything about God if He had not chosen to reveal Himself to us. So in those 1,900 names used of God and in those 20,000 references, just what does He tell us about Himself? We are told he is our healer, comforter, provider, saviour, all-sufficient, peace and protector. He is our righteousness and vindicator, defender of widows and orphans and committed partner for life and beyond. And that's just for starters. Oral Roberts is reputed to have said, "Every time God asks me to undertake a great task, He permits me to start with the same resources as He started with when he made the world – **nothing**!" But now, as then, God's Word works and unlocks His resources for every situation.

A friend of mine had been very successful in business and decided it was time to sell. He approached consultants specialising in his kind of business. They sent him and his directors home with a task to be done: they should prepare a business plan for three, five and ten years and then come back. Three months later they returned with the detailed proposals.

"You misunderstood," the consultants said. "We wanted you to develop the plans not with your funds, but with unlimited funds, as if a huge world player had bought you out. So they re-worked the plans and as a result he got seven times more for his company than he first thought.

"And it is he who will supply all your needs from his riches in glory, because of what Christ Jesus has done for us."

(PHILIPPIANS 4:19 LB)

START PRAYING FOR A PROBLEM!

Aren't we meant to pray for blessings? Besides we don't need to pray for problems they come along on their own, just like supermarket offers: two for the price of one! Of course, I don't mean we should pray to have problems, but we should pray for other people's problems.

Paul taught Titus to teach,

> *"Our people must also learn to engage in good deeds to meet pressing needs, so that they will not be unfruitful."*
>
> (TITUS 3:14 NASB)

People and organisations are the same, in that as time goes by they give more attention to what they were, rather than what they are becoming. God deals with us according to what He sees we are to become. And we are called to be a blessing to the planet as we walk in Abraham's calling.

> *"And in you all the families of the earth shall be blessed."*
>
> (GENESIS 12:3)

Abraham's grandson, Jacob, was a lying thief who took on a disguise to defraud a blind old man and stole from his own brother. You can read the story in Genesis. His brother Esau was mad enough to kill him and so Jacob ran, not returning home for twenty years. When he did return home, he sent a fortune in gifts ahead of himself to give to Esau. It took Jacob twenty years of hard labour serving his uncle Laban, who changed the terms and conditions of his wages ten times, in order to learn that he wasn't here to take, but to give. His future was to be a blessing and so God schooled him according to his destiny not according to his history.

Find a need and meet it, find a hurt and heal it. Mother Theresa said that we all have the opportunity to be great because we all have the opportunity to serve.

Two young brothers were squabbling over their mother's pancakes. "I want the first one!" each cried. Seeing the opportunity to provide a good moral lesson, mum said, "Boys, boys, if Jesus were here, He would say, 'You have the first one.' He would want us to prefer one another." After a few minutes silence and reflection, one boy said to the other, "You be Jesus, Jack!"

We always want someone else to play the Jesus part, but it truly is our privilege.

A mother collared Jesus one day and said, "When all this kingdom thing works out, will You give my boys the most important jobs in the new administration?" The Bible records that the other disciples were indignant, most likely because they wanted the jobs themselves. Jesus used the moment to teach them their true priorities using these famous words:

"Anyone wanting to be the greatest must be the least — the servant of all."

(MARK 9:35 LB)

I think this story is brilliant because Jesus didn't reprimand them for the desire to be great, just their methods and motives for getting there. The Bible refers to this James' commandment as the *"**great**"* commandment, not just the "good" commandment.

> **"It's a sin to be good**
> **when God has called you to be great."**
> (Thom Reiner)

When I was a lad, sometimes up to no good, my mother would say, "Be sure your sins will find you out!" thinking she was quoting the Bible. Do you think that verse is in the Bible? If so, who said it and why?

These words were spoken by Moses. What sin could be so awful to make the "meekest man in all the earth" mad enough to say to a whole tribe, "Be sure your sins will find you out"? Was it murder ... adultery ... idolatry? Was it complaining and grumbling – something the boys in Israel were pretty good at? No, Moses only used this phrase on one occasion and it was for the sin of *non-involvement* (Numbers 32:23) – a sin that is not even usually on our list of sins! Just as Israel were about to cross over into the Promised Land, two of the tribes said, "We're not going. We prefer this side of the Jordan." Moses quickly realised that meant a sixth of the fighting, worshipping army would be wiped out in one go. There were still Jericho's and the giants to take ahead and every person counted.

Seeing Moses' anger, however, the tribes relented and said, "OK, we will go and fight with our brothers and then come back." Then Moses uttered the serious warning, "If you don't, then be sure your sins will find you out."

In God's kingdom, non-involvement is not an option. Just as God has shown us amazing grace, we need to show grace to others and get involved with praying for their breakthrough, just as we have received our own.

Look Down on Yourself

"People do that all the time, don't they?" you may ask. Not in the way I'm suggesting here. Read on!

People often look inwardly on themselves and very often, when they do, they don't particularly like what they see. An honest assessment of our inner selves will reveal need, weakness, things that need to change, habits that need to be broken. Maybe they are haunted by the perpetual school teacher's voice: "Could do better, must try harder." They live in sin-consciousness. They thought that when they came to Jesus they would be free from guilt and shame and failure. But their experience of church has been that one set of rules have been exchanged for another and they continue to live in condemnation. Nothing leads to a paralysis of life or impotence of action like condemnation.

One author writing a report on Scottish culture for a newspaper painted a rather bleak view of society. She wrote that Scotland's new business birth rate is one of the worst in the world, that the level of mental and physical health is one of the lowest for a developed country, and she puts it all down to the mindset of the people. She blames a negative mindset which, she claims, has been largely created by Christian Calvinism – "a dour religion that enjoys beating people up, telling them they will amount to nothing, and that God is mad at them because of their sin." Admittedly, this lady claimed to be an atheist and completely failed to see that so many initiatives created for the greater good of society were birthed by Christians. However, there is some substance to her observations.

Instead of looking "in" on ourselves, we should look "down" on ourselves – that is, look down as though we were in Heaven, seeing ourselves as God sees us and looking from His perspective. Even though we fail in many ways and are wrought with conflicting emotions, we must stand by faith in the grace of God, secure in the knowledge of what He has said and done.

Jacob is a great illustration for us.

Jacob runs from his family home having lied, stolen and cheated his way into grabbing his brother's rightful inheritance. Blind old Isaac has unwittingly given the family fortune into the hands of the wrong son. Jacob runs for his life on his mother's advice. He stops overnight at a deserted place, exhausted, and meets God in his dreams. He calls the place "Bethel", meaning "House of God". If you or

I were God showing up in Jacob's life at this point, naturally speaking, what would we say to him?

"Jacob, I am really, really disappointed in you ... "

"Jacob, is this any way for a believer to live?"

Or even,

"Judgment is coming my boy ... "

Or,

"Got you, at last!"

Instead God says to him,

"I am GOD, the God of Abraham your father and the God of Isaac. I'm giving the ground on which you are sleeping to you and to your descendants. Your descendants will be as the dust of the Earth; they'll stretch from west to east and from north to south. All the families of the Earth will bless themselves in you and your descendants. Yes I will stay with you, I'll protect you wherever you go, and I'll bring you back to this very ground. I'll stick with you until I've done everything I promised you."

(GENESIS 28:13–15 MSG)

No wonder a slave trader and self-confessed rapist like John Newton wrote, "Amazing grace".

So often our theology is faulty and so our lives the poorer.

While we have already spoken in an earlier chapter about the fact that God disciplines His kids, the truth is, that is the last resort. God the Holy Spirit lives in us and at all times is working to convince us of who we are in Christ, of how much He is for us, the power at work within us and the potential achievable through us.

We can find but one verse in Scripture relating to the Holy Spirit's work in the world:

"And He, when He comes, will convict the world concerning sin and righteousness and judgment."

(JOHN 16:8 NASB)

But dozens of verses regarding His work in the believer:

"He will guide you into all truth."

(JOHN 16:13)

"It is the Spirit who gives life."

(JOHN 6:63)

"But the Helper, the Holy Spirit."

(JOHN 14:26)

"[He is] the Spirit of truth."

(JOHN 14:17)

And then we remember,

*"There is therefore now **no** condemnation to those who are in Christ Jesus."*

(ROMANS 8:1, emphasis added)

"He made Him who knew no sin to be sin for us, that we might become the righteousness of God in Him."

(2 CORINTHIANS 5:21)

It is not the Holy Spirit's voice that says to us, "You can do better, must try harder." He is telling us and convicting us of Christ and His work in us and for us.

Twice God wrote the Ten Commandments. Moses broke the first lot before they made it to the camp, because the people could not keep them. The second time they were placed in the ark, under the lid called the mercy seat. This lid was the shape of two angels facing each other. The priest would come and cover it with blood. God looked down on the Law, but only saw it through the blood-soaked mercy seat. When God looks down at us, He only sees us through Jesus' blood.

When we approach God, He is *not* aware of our sins. If He were, He would kill us. He is aware of the blood of Christ.

> *"And having been made perfect, He became to all those who obey Him the source of eternal salvation."*
>
> (HEBREWS 5:9 NASB)

The truth is, God does amazing things through very ordinary, imperfect people! This is what James meant when he said, "Look, Elijah was a man just like us!"

BE OPEN TO NUDGES

> **"I have learned that life's greatest moments evolve from simple acts of cooperation with God's mysterious promptings – nudges that always lean towards finding what's been lost and freeing what's been enslaved."**
>
> (Bill Hybels)

Think about it! God the Holy Spirit is in the world telling people they have a terminal problem and they had better find an answer fast. And God the Holy Spirit is in me telling me that I am empowered and authorised to act on His behalf. There is nothing He loves better than to bring these two parties together. When that happens it nearly always results in a defining moment in the life of some person.

I had been speaking at a University Christian Union event and arrived home very late. Tired, I made my way up the

stairs to my bed, being careful not wake the rest of the
house. Half-way up the staircase I heard God say to me, "Go
back into town and go to the fish and chip shop."

I decided I was tired, not hungry and would rather be in
my bed. But then I was sure I heard God say to me, "You
won't sleep." People sometimes say to me, "How do you
know it's God speaking to you?" Well, you usually know
it's God because so often you have already begun arguing
with Him!

Reluctantly, I got back in my car and drove into town, not
knowing exactly where I was going or which fish and chip
shop I was heading for, assuming it was still open at this
hour. I decided I would stop at the first open one I came to.
I pulled over, went inside, and thought that while I was
there I may as well do the British thing and buy some fish
and chips!

While fumbling for the change in my pocket I heard a
voice, "Andrew! I have been praying I would meet you."
Standing in the corner was a man I had met three months
earlier. He owned an antiques shop and I had been browsing
in his store. One thing had led to another and I told him
about the amazing life found in knowing Jesus. He was
pleasant and polite, but not interested. He had a business, a
girl and life was good. But in the three months since we'd
met his life had become a living hell. His business went bust,
his girl left him and he was totally helpless and depressed.
He remembered our conversation and recalled my first
name only, but had no idea how to find me, having lost the
business card I gave him.

In desperation he had prayed that we would meet again
that very day. He had decided that if we didn't, then there
could be no God and nothing left worth living for. He was
suicidal. On hearing all of this at 2.00am on a street corner
outside a fish and chip shop, I was dumbfounded in
amazement at how much God must love this guy, that He

would summon me to meet him in this way. The following Sunday the man gave his life to Christ in our Sunday meeting.

I have many stories like this, occasions when one thing leads to another and you just don't know where it will all end up. Praying simple prayers like, "Lord, please use me for good in the life of someone I meet today," always gets a result.

GET A BIGGER LIFE

Here's a story from the Old Testament.

> *"One day the group of prophets came to Elisha and told him, 'As you can see, this place where we meet with you is too small.'"*
> (2 KINGS 6:1 NLT)

These disciples of the prophet wanted a bigger house. There are big people in the world who are living in small houses, like a Genie in a lamp. They have tremendous power and potential, but it only comes out when they are rubbed up – usually the wrong way by challenging circumstances. So often we settle for less when there is so much more.

The Hebrew word used here, translated "limited", is *tsar* and can mean several things.

Firstly it means "limited". Have you got to the point where you know that you are limited? Limited in your finances? Limited in your expectations? So many Christians have reduced their walk with God to "keeping the rules". Every day is just the same.

Tsar can also mean "affliction, adversary, enemy or oppressor". Sometimes God takes stock of our lives and thinks it's time for us to get going, so He brings a shaking and stirring into our lives. We often need to be motivated like this, because we will too easily settle for alternatives. It's like the rancher who had a visit from his neighbour. When the neighbour turned up he noticed that the man's dog was sitting howling on the front porch. "Why is your dog howling?" he asked. "He's sitting on a rake," came the reply. "Then why doesn't he move?" the man retorted. "Because, it's easier to howl!"

Thirdly, *tsar* can mean pebble or sharp stone. Have you ever had a pebble in your sandal on the beach? Unless you remove it you end up walking with a limp. Some people, amazingly, don't get rid of the "pebbles" in their lives. Instead they learn to live with their limitations and adapt to them. As a result their thinking, attitudes and lifestyles are permanently disfigured. What could have been temporary has become a way of life. This is exactly what happened to the Israelites in the wilderness. A two-week journey turned into forty years.

It's time to get your faith moving.

How?

Make a move. The company of prophets who met with Elisha initiated a new house build. We read in the story that follows that one fellow went out and "borrowed" an axe. He was determined not to be left out. The word translated "borrow" means "to get hold of by passionate begging". How desperate are you for God? Are you longing, reaching, yearning and pressing in on Him?

"Draw near to God and He will draw near to you."

(JAMES 4:8)

Making a move can be risky. You don't know how things will all work out. All too often we live on borrowed opinions or borrowed identities. But we can borrow the stories of those who went before us and say, if God did it for them, then He can do it for me. This man went with a borrowed axe, but came back with his own personal miracle.

Secondly, go to the cross and find life. In this story we read that Elisha threw a stick into a pool and made the axe head float. Can iron float? No – it must have been a miracle. The stick represents the cross in my life. Paul said, "I preach Christ and Christ crucified" (see 1 Corinthians 1:23). Everything changes through the cross. Sinners become righteous, the sick become well, the shamed become honoured, and curses are exchanged for blessing, death for life. The cross is the great reversal. Can iron float? Yes, if it changes shape and becomes a ship. When the cross touches my life and I die to my own way, inexperience, weakness, limitation and fear, I change shape and float into a whole new day. There is a very big ocean out there.

Happy sailing.